East of the City

The London Docklands Story

James Bentley

First published in Great Britain in 1997 by
Pavilion Books Limited
London House
Great Eastern Wharf
Parkgate Road
London SW11 4NQ

Designed by Andrew Barron and
Collis Clements Associates

A CIP catalogue record for this book is
available from the British Library.

ISBN 1 86205 057 0

Printed and bound in Spain by Graficas
Reunidas, S. A.

2 4 6 8 10 9 7 5 3 1

This book may be ordered by post direct from
the publisher. Please contact the Marketing
Department. But try your bookshop first.

Contents

1981
July 1st

Parliament passes legislation creating the London Docklands Development Corporation with responsibility for regenerating 2063 hectares (5,100 acres) of former docks in East London

November

House builders Wimpey, Barratt, Broseley and Comben move onto 9-hectare (22-acre) site at Savage Gardens, Beckton, and start first private housing scheme in Docklands

1982
April 26th

195 hectares (482 acres) of vacant land on Isle of Dogs designated as an Enterprise Zone for 10 years, offering relaxed planning regime and fiscal benefits

September

Government announces support for Docklands Light Railway scheme

1983
April

LDDC supports STOLport (future London City Airport) proposals for the Royal Docks

July

LDDC publishes Accounts for its first full year which reveal that £42m spent, including £22m on infrastructure, involving 84 separate projects. Chairman Nigel Broackes writes that 'we have every confidence that regeneration will be largely achieved within the target of 10–15 years'

September

Princess Alexandra opens Enterprise Zone's 'Red brick Road' and ASDA superstore on the Isle of Dogs

November

British Telecom announce plans for providing a comprehensive fibre optic network in Docklands

Chronology

1984
January — Enterprise Zone provided with first public transport link via Docklands Clipper bus service to Mile End underground station

April — Parliamentary Bill to build first phase of Docklands Light Railway (DLR) from Tower Hill to Island Gardens and Stratford receives Royal Assent

December — Patrick Jenkin, Secretary of State for the Environment, inaugurates work on DLR

1985
May — Government approves plans for STOLport

December — Kenneth Baker, Secretary of State for the Environment, in a House of Commons speech states that, 'London Docklands is the most exciting example of urban regeneration in the world – it has attracted over £1b of private investment'

1986
July — LDDC unveils Docklands Highways programme

1987
July — Olympia & York sign Master Building Agreement with LDDC to provide 1.1m sq.m (12.2m sq.ft) of offices on 29-hectare (71-acre) site centered on Canary Wharf in the Enterprise Zone

August — HM The Queen opens the Docklands Light Railway

October — London City Airport opens with first commercial flight to Paris

1990
April — Contract let to extend DLR to Bank station in The City

November — Topping out ceremony of the tower at Canary Wharf carried out by Michael Portillo, Environment Minister

1991
July — DLR links to Bank station in The City

August — First companies move into Canary Wharf

September — Government approves runway extension at London City Airport

December — Lower Lea Crossing linking Isle of Dogs and Royal Docks opened by Roger Freeman, Transport Minister

1992
February — Sir George Young, Housing Minister, opens Winsor Park in Beckton – Britain's largest social housing scheme for ten years

March — HRH The Princess of Wales opens London City Airport runway extension and first jet service (to Zurich)

May — Olympia & York place Canary Wharf in administration

1993
May — The Prime Minister, John Major, opens Limehouse Link Tunnel and East India Dock Tunnel, marking completion of Docklands Highways

October	Canary Wharf taken out of administration
November	Canary Wharf banks agree to honour Olympia & York's commitment for a financial contribution to extension of Jubilee Line
December	The Prime Minister, John Major, starts work on Jubilee Line Extension

1994
January — HRH The Prince of Wales lends support for plan to build an Urban Village in West Silvertown

March — Environment Secretary, John Gummer, opens DLR Beckton extension and starts development of West Silvertown Urban Village

October — Bermondsey Riverside handed on to London Borough of Southwark commencing phased programme of de-designation of LDDC

1995
December — Beckton successfully de-designated and handed on to London Borough of Newham

1996
February — IRA bomb explodes at South Quay, Isle of Dogs, killing two people, injuring many more and creating extensive damage to businesses and homes

August — Pharmaceutical company, Norton Healthcare, announces proposed purchase of 10-hectare (25-acre) site in Royal Docks for its European head office

August — Citibank announces plans to build new UK headquarters of 46,450 sq.m (500,000 sq.ft) at Canary Wharf for 2,500 employees

September — Michael Heseltine, Deputy Prime Minister, starts construction work for £200m DLR Lewisham Extension

December — Lottery Sports Fund grants £8.9m for 2,000-metre (2,000-yard) international rowing course at Royal Albert Dock

Surrey Docks de-designated

1997
January — Wapping & Limehouse de-designated

February — LDDC announce highest office take-up in nine years with 1.3m sq.ft of offices let in 1996, highest recorded figure since 1987

October — Isle of Dogs de-designated

1998
March — LDDC completes its regeneration remit with de-designation of Royal Docks (31st March)

'Twas August, and the fierce sun overhead
Smote on the squalid streets of Bethnal Green,
And the pale weaver, through his windows seen
In Spitalfields, look'd thrice dispirited.

Matthew Arnold

Introduction

The lines are by Matthew Arnold, from his poem 'East London', published in 1867. Arnold could have pushed further eastwards to view yet more squalor and dereliction, but had he done so he would also have discovered proud families, their homes spotless refuges amidst grime, their men and womenfolk skilled at tasks which had made London the greatest port in the world.

When I began working on this book, Docklands had been remarkably regenerated thanks to an extraordinary body, the London Docklands Development Corporation, and its leaders and staff. Yet, as this book reveals, much remains to be done. One bonus to me of this uncompleted work was the chance to drive around some of the yet-to-be-developed areas to discover what they were once like.

As an historian I also found enormous pleasure in seeing the Docklands of the past alive architecturally in the present. Converting warehouses into new homes need not destroy the ambience of magical industrial architecture – and examples survive here of buildings whose like have been mostly lost elsewhere in this country.

Traversing Docklands, I would sometimes think of those who had travelled through it before me – particularly Charles Dickens. During the whole of Easter Monday the road to Greenwich, Dickens recorded, was in a state of perpetual bustle and noise. 'Cabs, hackney-coaches, 'shay' carts, coal wagons, stages, onmibuses, sociables, gigs, donkey-chaises... roll along at their utmost speed; the dust flies in clouds, ginger-beer corks go off in volleys, the balcony of every public-house is crowded with people, smoking and drinking, half the private houses are turned into tea-shops, fiddles are in great request, every little fruit-shop displays its stall of gilt and gingerbread and penny toys; turnpike men are in despair; horses won't go on, and wheels will come of; ladies in 'carawans' scream with fright at every fresh concussion, and their admirers find it necessary to sit remarkably close to them, by way of encouragement'.

Maybe Docklands is not quite so merry these days, but it is merry enough. East of the City, festivals proliferate And the waterside pubs (not to speak of those pubs that do not front the river) are filled with the most entertaining characters. Naturally, in researching this book I have had to spend time in many of these hostelries, coping with the gargantuan meals they serve. Those I have not had space to mention will, please, forgive me.

My own view is that the London Docklands Development Corporation should have had its life prolonged to the year 2000. But if that had happened, I should not have had the pleasure of writing this book.

James Bentley

In Xanadu did Kubla Khan

A stately pleasure-dome decree:

Where Alph, the sacred river, ran

Through caverns measureless to man

Down to a sunless sea.

So twice five miles of fertile ground

With walls and tower were girdled round:

And there were gardens bright with sinuous rills

Where blossom'd many an incense-bearing tree;

And here were forests ancient as the hills,

Enfolding sunny spots of greenery.

Samuel Taylor Coleridge

The Setting and its History

Opposite: **Two of Docklands' most notable sights, the 245-metre (804-foot)-high tower at Canary Wharf and Cascades, a luxury riverside residential block.**

Few would have supposed that the fragmentary poem published by Samuel Taylor Coleridge in 1816, under the title of 'Kubla Khan, or a Vision in a Dream', would ever be taken for a vision of London Docklands. Certainly no one would have done so in the 1960s and the 1970s, before the London Docklands Development Corporation was set up in 1981 to regenerate the whole area.

Yet Docklands can now begin to support the comparison. 'Twice five miles of fertile ground' comprehended Coleridge's Xanadu. Today's Docklands covers 22 square kilometres (8½ square miles). 'Meandering with a mazy motion,' wrote Coleridge of the River Alph. Through Docklands the River Thames meanders just so. And the region – equal in size, as Docklanders observe, to the City and the West End put together – has been and is being transformed under the leadership of the London Docklands Development Corporation from an increasingly miserable land into what is in many respects an earthly paradise.

London Docklands stretches 13 kilometres (8 miles) eastwards from Tower Bridge and London Bridge, on both sides of the River Thames, to beyond both Greenwich and the Thames Flood Barrier; each of these extremities, oddly enough, just outside the remit of the London Docklands Development Corporation. Because of its remit, much that was perishing between these extremities has been restored, and in some cases put to new uses. These legacies of the past are in many respects unique survivals of a remarkable long-gone culture. In Docklands, the past shines through its topography, its docks, its canals and architecture. Hence my desire to set out at the beginning of this book the historical legacy which the LDDC inherited.

We begin our journey in the west. Tower Bridge, built as the sole major bridge spanning the river below London Bridge, is a miracle of engineering. Its creators, who began work in 1884, were the architect Sir Horace Jones and the engineer John Wolfe-Barry. They designed a bascule bridge, with twin drawbridges raised by counterpoise. Their commission required them to build a bridge whose headroom would reach 41 metres (135 feet) and whose span would be 61 metres (200 feet). They were also instructed to build in the Gothic style.

In 1894 the Prince of Wales officially opened Tower Bridge – its stone-clad towers framed in steel and weighty enough to support the massive bascules. Lattice girders hold up the decks. Hydraulic machinery (replaced in 1976 with electrically operated machines) raised and lowered the bridge. And lifts were installed, to carry pedestrians up and down from the footbridge which they could use when the bridge had been raised.

Left: **Tower Bridge, the 'gateway' to Docklands, is a masterpiece of late-Victorian engineering and architecture designed by John Wolfe Barry (son of the architect of the Houses of Parliament) and Sir Horace Jones.**

then – after he refused to allow his supporters to pay a ransom – beat him to death. Other acts of viciousness followed. Almost certainly the young King Henry VI, founder of King's College, Cambridge, and Eton College, Windsor, was murdered here in 1473. Here were born Henry VIII, Mary Tudor and Elizabeth I. Here Elizabeth I signed the order for the execution of Mary,

At the opposite end of the winding Thames which threads its way through Docklands is Greenwich, now readily accessible as a result of the Docklands Light Railway, one of the LDDC's prime achievements. For centuries the home of monarchs because of its easy access by water, Greenwich, set on a ridge overlooking the river, is now an exquisite ensemble of seventeenth- and eighteenth-century buildings.

Its past has been historically redolent and at times murky. When the Danes captured Alfege, Archbishop of Canterbury, in 1012, they imprisoned him at Greenwich and

Queen of Scots. Here in 1756 Admiral John Byng, who had failed to relieve Minorca when it was besieged by a French fleet, was imprisoned before his execution for neglect of duty. Here, after his death at the battle of Trafalgar, Horatio Nelson's body lay in state before sailing up the river in a royal barge to be buried in St Paul's Cathedral.

A royal abode has stood at Greenwich certainly since the early fifteenth century. The first major palace was built for Duke Humphrey of Gloucester, the regent of the boy-king Henry VI. The regent also enclosed the 77 hectares (190 acres) of Greenwich Park. Subsequently, for over two hundred years Greenwich was the home of the monarchs of England (and then of England and Scotland), till 1629.

Indeed it was their chief home, comprising a tilting ground and an armoury. Close by, presaging the rise of the London docks, were the naval dockyards of Woolwich and Deptford.

In 1605 James I, son of Mary, Queen of Scots, gave the palace and park to his wife Anne of Denmark. Eleven years later he commissioned Inigo Jones to design the first of the surviving buildings of Greenwich. King James intended to present the building to his wife, but the Queen's House was not finished until 1637, 18 years after her death, and became the home of her daughter-in-law Henrietta Maria, wife of King Charles I. Inigo Jones himself described this Palladian building as 'sollid, proporsionable according to the rulles, masculine and unaffected'.

Here Charles I and his Queen spent their last night together, on 11 February 1642. Its Great Hall – a perfect cube, measuring 12.2 metres (40 feet) by 12.2 metres by 12.2 metres – boasts what is probably the first spiral staircase constructed in Britain (it was known as the tulip staircase), as well as superb frescoes painted by Sir James Thornhill in the second quarter of the eighteenth century. (Thornhill charged £1 a foot for the walls and £3 a foot for the ceiling.) And symmetrical colonnades flank either side of this exquisite, former royal home.

Below: A closer look at Greenwich, in whose design some of the most noted British architects had a hand – including Inigo Jones, Sir Christopher Wren, Nicholas Hawksmoor and Sir John Vanbrugh.

Opposite: Looking across the Thames to Greenwich, in its time home to a royal residence, an observatory and a hospital for retired and sick seamen.

17

Charles I lost his head in the Civil War, and his palace became one of the residences of Oliver Cromwell. When Charles II, the son of the executed monarch, managed to succeed to the throne, the new King had the ancient palace demolished. In the middle of its park, in 1675, King Charles II founded the Royal Observatory.

One curiosity of this observatory is the Greenwich meridian. For centuries most countries used their own capital city as the zero point from which they measured longitude. Only in 1884, at an international conference held in Washington, did the maritime nations of the world meet to discuss where an agreed zero line of longitude should run. They chose Greenwich. The spot also demarcated Greenwich Mean Time, on which the time throughout the rest of the world is based. Today the zero meridian of longitude is marked at intervals throughout this part of Docklands. Across it visitors straddle, one foot in the eastern hemisphere, one in the western.

Charles II also desired a new palace to match Inigo Jones's Queen's House. Nothing came of this plan, but in 1694 Queen Anne commissioned Christopher Wren to develop the site as a hospital for retired and sick seamen. Wren offered to work for nothing. His assistant was Nicholas Hawksmoor, and the project was finished by the brilliant baroque architect Sir John Vanbrugh.

It reappears, audibly, with the Greenwich Time Ball. In 1833 the Lords Commissioners of the Admiralty gave notice, that, to apprise mariners of the correct time, 'a ball will hence forward be dropped, every day, from the top of a pole on the eastern turret of the Royal Observatory at Greenwich, at the moment of one-o'-clock p.m. solar time.' Each day, at 1.00 p.m. Greenwich Mean Time, the red time ball is still dropped.

Some two hundred years ago Canaletto painted this ensemble of splendid buildings, from across the river. Remarkably, standing at Island Gardens on the Isle of Dogs, from where Canaletto took his perspective, you see virtually what he painted, still today unspoilt.

Greenwich also boasts a baroque church, St Alfege, dedicated to the archbishop and martyr, who owed his death in part to the Thames, for the invading Danes who killed him had arrived by river. The original church was destroyed by a storm in the early eighteenth century. The parishioners were too poor to restore it themselves, and they begged Parliament to levy a tax on coal to finance the rebuilding. Their wish was granted, and St Alfege was rebuilt, for the most part between 1711 and 1714, by Nicholas Hawksmoor, whose churches also enhance parts of Docklands (and have been restored in part through the initiatives of the LDDC). Ultimately, some 50 such 'coal' churches were built, making this a remarkable Queen Anne pioneer.

Above left: **A bustling river scene from the early 1930s. At this time London was still one of the world's major ports.**
Right: **Past and present: A derelict industrial site on the Isle of Dogs allows a tantalizing glimpse of Greenwich's elegant buildings.**

In spite of being damaged by enemy bombs during the Second World War, St Alfege has been restored to much of its former nobility. Its tower and spire, added by the architect John James in 1730, seem, by contrast to Hawksmoor's work, feeble (to use an adjective of no less an authority than John Betjeman). The site is historic. On this spot, in the predecessor to Hawksmoor's church, Henry VIII and Elizabeth I were baptized. Buried here is Major James Wolfe, hero of the siege of Quebec in 1759. He had sailed from here and returned dead and embalmed.

Greenwich offers visitors a final reminder of the long-past seafaring life of London's docklands with the *Cutty Sark*, which was brought here in 1954. The last and certainly the most famous of the tea-clippers, this elegant vessel, whose name derives from Robert Burns's 'Tam O'Shanter', was built at Dumbarton in 1869 for a London shipowner. She now houses a collection of ships' painted and carved figureheads. In her working days the *Cutty Sark* could carry 2,972 square metres (32,000 square feet) of sail and reach a speed of 17½ knots.

Today visitors to Greenwich arrive easily from the heart of London by taking the Docklands Light Railway to Island Gardens, and then walking through the Greenwich Tunnel (although by the year 2000 the DLR will have been extended to Greenwich and Lewisham). The Greenwich Tunnel was constructed at the turn of the present century by Sir Alexander Binnie to replace a ferry that had plied the Thames since 1676, and is again a reminder of the heyday of London's docks, for its initial purpose was to be a pedestrianized way for dockers employed in the West India Docks.

Arriving here, visitors should muse on Dr Samuel Johnson's verse (he lodged for a time in Church Street, Greenwich):

*On Thames's banks in silent thought
    we stood:
Where Greenwich smiles upon the silver
    flood:
Pleased with the seat which gave
    Eliza birth,
We kneel and kiss the consecrated earth.*

Not surprisingly, then, did William Hazlitt note that for the true Cockney, 'Greenwich Park stands him in stead of the Vales of Arcady.'

Right: **Small terraced houses in Saville Road, Silvertown, are dwarfed by the massive passenger liner *Dominion Monarch*, in a photograph taken in 1950 when the ship was in dry dock.**

Towards the eastern extremity of Docklands is the Thames Flood Barrier, designed to protect London from rare but potentially lethal high tides. London has always been susceptible to flooding. To give two examples: as long ago as 1099 the *Anglo-Saxon Chronicle* recorded a disastrous flood; and on 7 December 1663 Samuel Pepys recorded that overnight had

devastating flood of water likely to surge up the Thames are a trough of low pressure across the Atlantic and northerly gales.

A number of people had urged the building of a barrier across the Thames, and as early as 1904 a Thames Barrage Association had been formed. Barriers had

occurred 'the greatest tide that ever was remembered in England to have been in this river, all Whitehall being drowned'.

In attempts to quell the floods, walls and embankments were built, particularly after the Thames Flood Act of 1879, but these precautions were often insufficient. Floods recurred; buildings were inundated; men and women drowned. In 1828, for example, 14 people in Westminster drowned in a flood. In 1853 some 300 were drowned in a flood along the east coast of England and the estuary of the Thames.

That a yet more disastrous flood would inevitably one day occur was now clear, for several inexorable reasons. First, London is built on clay and is slowly sinking. Secondly, the whole of Britain is tilting imperceptibly towards the south-east. Thirdly, with the melting of the polar ice caps, the volume of water in the Atlantic is gradually rising. Finally, the conditions required to create a

even been designed. An inquiry held after the 1953 flooding seriously recommended building one, but nothing happened until the passing of the Thames Barrier and Flood Prevention Act in 1972. Within three years of the Act construction had begun of an immense 520-metre (1,706-foot) barrier across the river, with no fewer than ten shipping gates.

The area that lies broadly within the boundaries of London Bridge/Tower Bridge, Greenwich and the Thames Flood Barrier is London Docklands, known till very recently by those who worked there simply as 'the docks'. They date back to Saxon times, possibly even earlier, though there is no solid evidence to support this thesis. Certainly the Saxons and Romans dug watery alleyways in the banks of the Thames and buttressed them with stakes. And certainly Roman ships sailed the Thames. Whether these Romans built docks we do not yet know.

Above: An aerial view of the Royal Docks and the Thames Barrier. Completed in 1982 at a cost of £435 million, the barrier is a feat of engineering equalling that of Tower Bridge at the opposite end of Docklands.
Right: The Thames winds around the showpiece of regenerated Docklands, Canary Wharf Tower. In the foreground on the right is the 'coal' church of St George in the East, Wapping.

Above: The River
Thames meanders
through Docklands.
Clearly visible north
of the river are Royal
Victoria Dock, Royal
Albert Dock and King
George V Dock, as are
the docks of the
Isle of Dogs and
Greenland Dock to
the west.

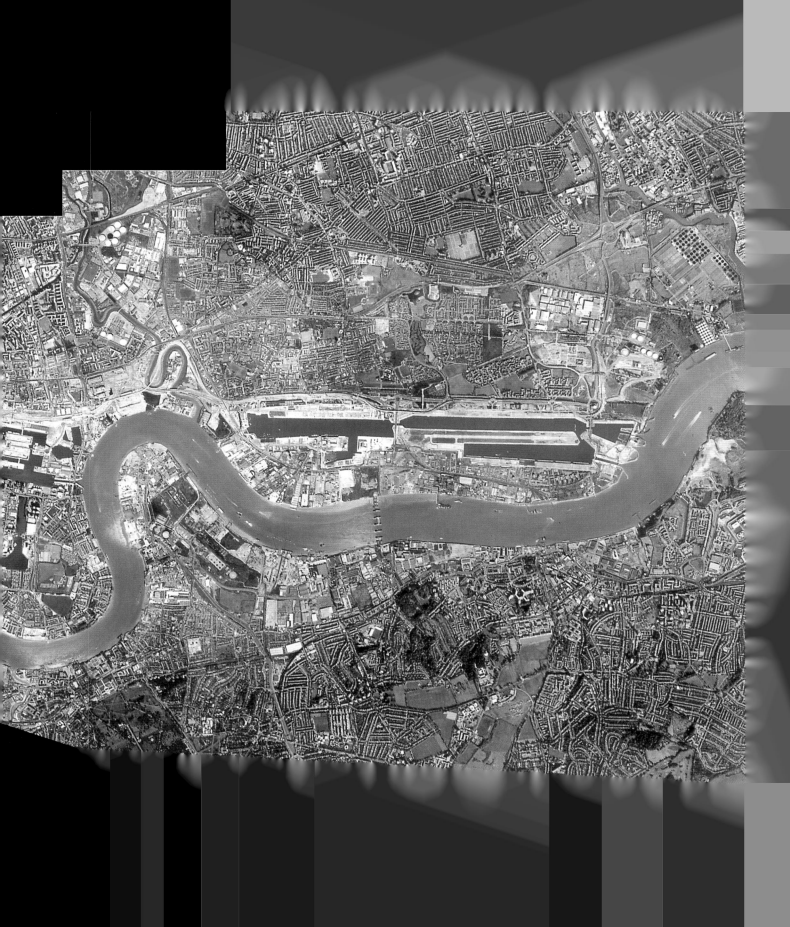

The first monarch to take a really keen interest in the capital's docklands was probably, and not surprisingly, Queen Elizabeth I – for after all, she owed her throne and probably her life to her navy, which had defeated the Spanish Armada. She decreed that all ships docking at London should unload under supervision at 17 specially designated quays. A couple more docks were created in the seventeenth century, but after that the excavation of docks in London virtually ceased for a hundred years.

Yet the port of London flourished. In 1699 a wharf for fisherfolk was founded at Billingsgate, whose market transferred to the Isle of Dogs, to a 5.4-hectare (13½-acre) site in the West India Docks, on 19 January 1982. This was and remains a celebrated fish market, dating back at least to the early eleventh century. After the battle of Agincourt, the porters decided to wear hats modelled on those of the English archers (a habit sadly discontinued). By an Act of Parliament of 1698 anyone was allowed to sell fish there, not just (as hitherto) a tight cabal of fishmongers. Many times enlarged, it still continued to prove too small, hence the transfer – at a cost of £11 million.

A visit to the new Billingsgate is a treat. It has a quaintly pleasing weathervane in the shape of a fish. A copy of the clock from old Billingsgate graces the main market hall. By its charter the traders have to sell to retail as well as wholesale customers. One snag from the point of view of the general public is that it is open only from 4.30 a.m. till 8.30 a.m. Another snag is that the porters scarcely care about visitors, who must watch out for physical injury as the porters' trucks speed heedlessly by.

As for the delightfully named Isle of Dogs, this is really a peninsula, not an island, created on the north bank of the Thames above Greenwich by a great loop of the river. Only when the West India Docks were built across it did part of the Isle of Dogs truly constitute an island.

In medieval times the Isle of Dogs was known as Stepney Marsh, and in the thirteenth century parts were drained to support meadows and pastures as well as cornfield. Unfortunately, in 1448 the embankment of Deptford broke, Stepney Marsh was submerged and its prosperous small community had to leave.

Only 140 years later does the name Isle of Dogs appear on any map, perhaps because there had been royal kennels here. But by now scarcely anyone lived on the inhospitable peninsula – a mere 4,000 according to the census of 1851, and that was after the development of the docks was attracting immigrants from other parts of Great Britain. But William Cubitt, who was to become Lord Mayor of London in 1860 and 1861, had the foresight in the mid-nineteenth century to develop a town on the south-east tip of the Isle. Not only did he build a church; his servants set up sawmills, potteries, brick fields, timber wharves and even a cement factory. Interestingly, the pattern of the streets of Cubitt Town was laid out along the pattern of the former drainage ditches.

Left: **Millwall Dock was entered by a lock constructed in the mid–1860s; at that time it was the largest lock in** **Docklands. Badly damaged during World War II, the dock has been sensitively restored.**

remain immobile for up to two months, while their cargoes were unloaded. It is estimated that a third of the dock labour force in the late eighteenth century consisted of thieves or receivers of stolen goods. Gangs of thieves were brilliantly organized, some operating by night, others by day. In consequence the losses suffered by the river traffic were massive.

Yet the docks had begun to flourish earlier. In the early eighteenth century Daniel Defoe recorded that the ships powered by sail numbered here around two thousand. In addition he described barges and lighters, as well as pleasure boats, sailing the Thames. Defoe discovered 33 shipyards where ships were built, three wet docks where they were laid up and another 22 dry docks where they were repaired.

Till the eighteenth century the Thames had long been a major thoroughfare into England's capital. Its traffic was also prey to piracy and thieves, for there were scarcely any warehouses (save those housing tobacco) to store goods. River congestion now forced many vessels to

In 1798 merchants of the West India Company, whose annual losses from pilfering were then reaching £150,000, approached a celebrated advocate of river police, the Glaswegian Dr Patrick Colquhoun. Once Lord Provost of Glasgow, Colquhoun had been appointed a London magistrate and in 1795 had written *A Treatise on the Police of the Metropolis*. On behalf of the company, which funded it, he set up a force of some two hundred men, run by a clerk, a chief constable and a permanently available magistrate. Most of them were watermen, those who ferried passengers along the Thames. A few were lightermen, those who bore the ships' loads to the quayside. Some were seamen. All were armed, and they often had to fight vicious battles with the pilferers.

Colquhoun's force was eventually united with the Metropolitan police. And another measure was to insist that those who

unloaded goods from the vessels of the East India Company wear specially designed uniforms in which no one could hide pilfered goods.

But these draconian measures failed to stamp out pilfering. So the seafaring traders eventually thought it wise to protect their cargoes by building enclosed docks. (They then hired their own police forces, until these all merged with the officers of the Port of London Authority in 1909.) The basic materials for these docks were always there. Two hundred years ago, when they were first developed, this was marshland, ideal for creating docks, since the moment anyone digs a hole it fills with water. So enclosed docks were created, the first in 1802, the last in 1921. Three dry docks remain: a couple at Blackwall Yard in Poplar and the third at Nelson Dock in Southwark.

Instantly it was perceived that unless retaining walls were built, the river would swamp the marshland which surrounds it. Dockland retaining walls were therefore built, and those still remaining are now recognized as important examples of British industrial architecture and in many cases are preserved with the help of the London Docklands Development Corporation. These walls gave names to such places as Millwall, Blackwall and Wapping Wall. Under the stimulus of the

Opposite: In the past, West India Dock could shelter some 600 ships. Opened in 1802, it stretched for 0.8km (½ mile) and was protected from pilferers by virtually impenetrable walls.

Below: In 1929 the passenger liner *Oronsay* enters New Entrance Lock at Tilbury. With the advent of containerisation, Tilbury was to become a major competitor of the London docks.

2 9

LDDC, such docks are now prized sites, for homes and leisure developments, for shops and restaurants.

Watermen and dockers reached the river by stairs, some of which still access the stone hards which appear at low tide. They were reached (and in some cases still are) by tunnels either between or through the warehouses. Once more, these are nowadays recognized as prime survivors of an industrial era now past.

In Wapping the walls of London Docks survive. So do the 1890s' walls of Surrey Docks, once almost derelict, now decently repaired. And when new buildings were designed for Heron Quays, care was taken to preserve the splendid walls of the West India Export Docks.

The West India Company was one of the first companies to set about building docks on a large scale. Vessels moored in its docks were protected from the tides by locks. Next came London Docks, in 1805, with the East India Dock constructed later in the same year. In 1807 Surrey Commercial Dock was excavated on the south bank of the Thames. Then came St Katharine Docks in 1828, West India South a year later, Royal Victoria in 1853, Millwall in 1868, Royal Albert in 1880 and King George V in 1921.

These enclosed docks were magnificent specimens of industrial architecture. To store goods and yet have them readily loaded for transportation, dock warehouses needed to be accessible throughout the whole length of the ground floor, so eventually the buildings were divided only by colonnades. These docks were a source of national pride. The Prime Minister himself, William Pitt, was present in 1800 when the foundation stone of the West India Dock was laid.

The West India Company was not so rich as the East India Company. Founded in 1600, the East India Company had, during the reign of Charles II, built a small dock at Blackwall covering 0.6 hectares (1½ acres). As Secretary to the Navy, Samuel Pepys visited the dock in 1661 and noted with delight *The Royal Oak*, a new merchant vessel built there. In 1789 this dock (used only for building and fitting ships and not for handling cargoes) was enlarged to become Brunswick Dock, so named in honour of George III.

By this time the East India Company had grown rich and influential – importing tea and porcelain from China, and from India more tea, as well as spices, indigo and silks. It had set up factories in India and in the eighteenth century virtually controlled much of that country. Its vessels were the largest using the port of London. Many of them were built here in the Blackwall Shipyard, which set up business in the late sixteenth century. Some large ships could moor at Blackwall Reach, but for the most part the vessels of the company sailed as far as Deptford.

By the time the docklands were being exploited, the company already possessed magnificent London warehouses. In 1803 the East India Company decided to obtain an Act of Parliament to construct new docks. The engineers John Rennie and Ralph Walker oversaw the work, which was so speedily completed that the new docks (which incorporated Brunswick Dock) opened three years later. A locked basin connected the Thames with a 7.3-hectare (18-acre) import dock and a much smaller export dock.

Left above: The last of the great docks, King George V Dock, in 1980.
Right: A model of the West Indiaman *Hibbert* tops the principal gateway of West India Docks, as it was c. 1930.

THE OLD GATEWAY — WEST INDIA DOCKS

Rennie and Walker had already worked on the still finer docks of the West India Company, under the brilliant designer William Jessop, builder of the Grand Union Canal. Their aim was to cut down dramatically the time taken to discharge cargoes – from four weeks to a breathless four days. Constructed on the Isle of Dogs after an Act of Parliament of 1799, the docks were begun in 1800 and opened in 1802.

The Act laid down rules: the docks, quays and warehouses must be surrounded by a brick or stone wall, at least 9 metres (30 feet) high, outside which there had to be a kind of moat – a ditch 3.6 metres (12 feet) wide, 1.8 metres (6 feet) deep and always filled with water.

By 1802 Jessop had fulfilled his commission, designing an import dock of 12 hectares (30 acres) and an export dock of 9.7 hectares (24 acres). Two basins, one at either end of the docks and connected to them by locks, gave access to the Thames, also via locks. The export dock was surrounded by warehouses five storeys high and stretching continuously for 1.2 kilometres (three-quarters of a mile).

Ships berthed by way of the Blackwall shore of the Isle of Dogs; lighters entered by way of Limehouse. So successful were these docks that within three years a canal was dug, linking them with Blackwall and Wapping – a waterway which at the end of the 1860s was transformed into the South West India Dock.

Today a statue of Robert Milligan, who was Deputy Chairman of the company when work began, stands outside the Grade I listed Ledger Building, at the western end of the sugar warehouses at West India Quay. It was sculpted after his death in 1809 by Robert Westmacott, moved in 1875 and brought back to its original site by the LDDC only in 1997.

London Docks at Wapping came into business three years after the opening of the West India Docks. Once again the docks were divided into two, the smaller eastern dock covering 2.8 hectares (7 acres) and spilling into the Thames through a basin and locks, the larger western dock comprising 8 hectares (20 acres) and also connected to the river with a basin and locks. The little Tobacco Dock connected the two.

Daniel Alexander, surveyor to Trinity House, is credited with their construction, but in fact much of the work was done by John Rennie, who had served as a consultant to William Jessop when he was designing the West India Docks. Brick warehouses, four storeys high, whose stone plinths and rustications were carved with ammonites, rose above brick-vaulted wine cellars. The company relished for 21 years its near monopoly of the rice, tobacco, wine and brandy trade with London, as well as the profits from its splendid woollen warehouse.

Right: **Surrey Docks today comprises homes, a watersports centre and a yacht marina. Prominent on the left of the picture is Baltic Quay, with its fourteen-storey tower and barrel-vaulted residential quarters.**

In 1807 Surrey Commercial Dock was built, 3.2 kilometres (2 miles) east of London Bridge on the south bank of the Thames (its name was later changed to the plural, as more docks were added). A dock had existed here since the late seventeenth century, built on behalf of a rich Streatham landowner named James Howland. Begun in 1695 and opened in 1700, Howland's Dock was rectangular in shape and huge for that era. A total of 120 merchant ships could moor at its quays, all of them protected from winds by rows of trees. (Howland's Dock was renamed Greenland Dock in 1763, after the Arctic whalers who used it as a base.) Surrey Commercial Dock, which in fact consisted of nine enclosed docks and a canal, based itself on Howland's great dock. The whole complex prospered in the eighteenth and early nineteenth centuries, chiefly on whaling, supplying oil for example to London's 5,000 whale-oil lamps. As well as thriving as the largest whale dock in the world, these harbours also prospered on shipbuilding and on the import from the Baltic of timber (eventually becoming the largest timber port in the world). Grain too was a major import, while the coal trade was another element in its life. And at the beginning of the twentieth century cold stores were built here to safeguard dairy products, and the complex was enlarged, to cover 8.8 hectares (22 acres) and accommodate bigger ships. Amid the traditional docks, it was an oddity, and was owned by four separate companies.

Below: Splendidly restored, Greenland Dock, Rotherhithe, once sheltered Arctic whalers. Now the site of a marina and watersports centre, Greenland Dock is surrounded by homes.

In the view of Charles Dickens, the citizens of this part of the docklands were a colourful, sometimes unsavoury lot. 'Jostling with unemployed labourers of the lowest class, balast heavers, coal whippers, brazen women,' he felt himself assailed by offensive sights and smells from narrow alleys. He perceived 'stacks of warehouses that rise from every corner'.

The area was savagely bombed in 1940, the timber set on fire creating the largest conflagration ever seen in Britain since the Great Fire of London. Although the docks were in part restored after the Second World War, inevitably they shared the fate of the rest of London's docklands and were closed down in 1970.

Right: The tree-shaded walkway alongside Greenland Dock, where as part of its restoration willows, Italian alders and eucalyptus trees have been planted – similar to those which served as wind-breaks here in the eighteenth century.

Below: The gates of
Millwall Docks, under
construction and
almost ready for use
in 1868. Beyond
them the dock walls
can be seen.

Below: The gates of Millwall Docks, under construction and almost ready for use in 1868. Beyond them the dock walls can be seen.

MILLWALL DOCK.

St Katharine Docks' name derives from the twelfth-century church of St Katharine, which, ironically, was demolished (along with the homes of over 11,000 people) when the basin and two docks were created in 1828. Two skilled industrial architects, Thomas Telford and Philip Hardwick, co-operated in its construction. They designed yellow-brick warehouses (many of them, unfortunately, now demolished), which were supported on Doric columns made of iron, their walls pierced by segment-headed openings. Here were unloaded cargoes of tea and rubber, sugar and tallow, matches, wool and marble. And in 1864 these docks amalgamated with London Docks. After their closure in 1968, vessels from the Maritime Trust's collection were brought here, most notably Captain Scott's *Discovery*.

The marshes on the western side of the Isle of Dogs took the name Millwall from seventeenth- and eighteenth-century mills which were used to drain the land. In 1864 the Millwall Freehold Land and Dock Company moved into action, buying around 80 hectares (200 acres) of marshy land south-west of the West India Docks on the Isle of Dogs. Four years later its newly constructed Millwall Dock, built to designs by John Fowler and William Wilson and covering 14.5 hectares (36 acres) of water, with a dry dock 126 metres (413 feet) long, was already trading, particularly in grain from the Baltic. In 1909 it was linked to South Quay and the West India Docks.

Finally the Royal Docks were inaugurated. Nowhere else in the world do any docks exceed their combined size of 99 hectares (245 acres). Of all the London docks they lie closest to the sea, a strategic position which allowed them to welcome the largest ocean-going ships. Royal Victoria Dock was the first to be built, on behalf of the St Katharine Dock Company, and the first to cater for iron steamships. Opened by the sovereign's consort Prince Albert in 1855, Royal Victoria Dock was marvelled at for its hydraulic lifts and cranes. It was extended east to create the Royal Albert Dock, designed by Sir Alexander Rendel and opened by the Duke of Connaught in 1880. This dock was even larger than the Victoria, stretching for 1.2 kilometres (three-quarters of a mile), its quayside reaching another 4.8 kilometres (3 miles). The two of them together boast 70 hectares (175 acres) of water and a quayside 11 kilometres (7 miles) long.

Below: Since 1973, after over a century of trading, St Katharine Docks has served as a yacht haven.

37

Then in 1912 the engineer Frederick Palmer began work on King George V Dock, which – delayed by the First World War – was opened in 1921. King George V Dock comprises 18 hectares (45 acres) of water. Here, on 6 August 1939, the 35,665-tonne *Mauretania* edged itself precariously into the dock. One hundred thousand people gathered to watch the feat. Owing to the danger that on its next attempt to dock this great ship might not enter unscathed, the feat was never repeated.

Many of these improvements survived the war years. But then the docks went into decline. The port of Liverpool was a damaging competitor, as were Southampton, Felixstowe and Harwich. The British empire was fading away, and so too was protected trade. New container-ships were not designed for these old, once state-of-the-art docks. The Port of London Authority attempted to fight back by moving the bulk of trade down the river to Tilbury, where more up-to-date facilities had been built. So in the late 1970s and early 1980s London's historic dockyards finally, reluctantly closed. With them declined a once (though not always) thriving and in many ways vibrant community.

When the London Docklands Development Corporation took responsibility for the region, its remit, like that of Kubla Khan, was to create a Xanadu out of this once flourishing, now sadly worn-out land. Set up in 1981, it was to be funded with government grants and was given the right to sell off disused docks and redundant land. Yet its mission was from the start one of regeneration as well as conservation. Historic buildings, their essential character preserved, were to be utilized for new purposes. The LDDC was charged by Parliament with what many might have regarded as an impossible dream: the 'permanent' regeneration of Docklands.

The Thames was still a sacred river. Here were needed, in Coleridge's words, stately pleasure domes, walls and towers, girdled around with gardens bright with sinuous rills, where blossomed incense-bearing trees and forests enfolding sunny spots of greenery.

The LDDC set about achieving exactly that. But the physical legacy it had inherited was dire. Moreover, people had moved out, drawn to richer areas and new towns. And little wonder. Much of the housing in Docklands was still, in the judgement of one LDDC Chief Executive (Michael Honey), 'substandard'. Health and education provision was also poor. The Labour government admitted this in its White Paper 'Policy for the Inner Cities' in 1977. 'Many of the inner areas surrounding the centres of our cities suffer from economic decline, physical decay and adverse social conditions,' it declared. It also had a vision and a dire warning. 'The inner parts of our cities ought not to be left to decay. It would

Left above:
On 6 August 1939, at the end of her maiden voyage, SS *Mauretania* gingerly edges into King George V Lock, a feat never repeated. *Left below:* Wharfside cranes at Royal Victoria Dock.

Right: The massive Royal Victoria Dock, looking west. In past times, rows of ships, sometimes three deep, would line the quayside here.

Two years after the publication of the White Paper, the Labour government was replaced by a Conservative administration. In those two years money had been pumped into urban programmes, using local government as the chief agencies. Now, with the new government came new ideas. As Secretary of State for the Environment, Michael Heseltine was

mean leaving large numbers of people to face a future of declining job opportunities, a squalid environment, deteriorating houses and declining public services.'

The White Paper was also pessimistic. 'Some of the changes that have taken place are due to social and economic forces which could be reversed only with great difficulty or at an unacceptable cost.' Clearly, however, matters could not be left as they stood. The White Paper looked to local authorities as the chief agencies for regeneration, with some input from voluntary groups and the private sector. The authors were clear not only that in some way the economy of the inner cities needed to be strengthened but also that both the physical aspect and environment had to be improved.

By now the docks were isolated from the heart of London, not only physically and in terms of transport systems, but also psychologically. It seemed clear to many docklanders that they were not really part of the burgeoning expansion of London; that they need not even apply for jobs there.

Left: An early 1980s view across the 1.6 hectares (4 acres) of water of Limehouse Basin (also known as Regent's Canal Dock).

Above right: Blue Bridge, spanning the West India Docks entrance. The bridge was based on Dutch models and was built by the Port of London Authority in 1969 to replace an older swing bridge.

particularly keen to bring about much greater involvement by the private sector. This, it was recognized, could best be achieved by easing planning regulations and also by selling to the private sector public land for its developments.

In 1980 the Local Government Planning and Land Act was passed, with provisions to create new Urban Development Corporations. In spring 1981, the first was established for Merseyside. In the summer of that year another was established for Docklands. Eventually, as the LDDC and Merseyside UDC flourished, the government set up another nine Urban Development Corporations throughout the country.

On 2 July 1981 the London Docklands Development Corporation became a legal entity, with an estate of 116 hectares (287 acres). Reg Ward, its shadow Chief Executive for the previous year, now took on the role formally. It was time for a new start. Yet Reg Ward had what many considered an unenviable job, tackling a seemingly impossible task ...

2

O fruitful genius! that bestowest here
An everlasting plenty year by year;
O place! O people! manners, framed to please
All nations, customs, kindreds, languages!

Robert Herrick

A New Start

Opposite: **Hay's Galleria rises where tea clippers used to dock at Hay's Wharf. The Galleria is breathtakingly elegant, with its domed glass roof and impressive fountain.**

Below: **In the early 1950s the Royal Docks were thriving, helping to maintain London's status as one of the world's major ports.**

Robert Herrick's verses on London bespeak the riches already brought to the city by the Thames in the seventeenth century. Many years later, writing in 1943, Sir Patrick Abercrombie described the Thames, by virtue of its great width, its sweeping and varied curves, its tidal ebb and flow and its shipping activities, as one of the finest rivers in the world. 'It presents unequalled opportunities for public enjoyment,' he continued; 'it makes London the first port of Great Britain; as a great waterway it provides a cheap means of freight transport and it is the backbone of London's industrial areas.'

For as long as it was a city, London was also a port. Overseas trade blossomed spectacularly during the seventeenth and eighteenth centuries. It scarcely ceased throughout seven decades of the twentieth century. From London Bridge to the sea, the Port of London Authority dredged 80 kilometres (50 miles) of the Thames, to allow modern ocean-going ships passage to the Port of London. By 1939 cargo passing through the docks amounted to 60 million tonnes.

Coastal services, short-sea trading, storage, trade in grain, sugar, hardwood, tea, wool, wine and spirits, silk and feathers, cigars and tobacco, wheat,

lumber, drugs, frozen meat, bananas and the rest made this the world's premier port. The central granary at Millwall Docks could accommodate 24,000 tonnes of grain. The Royal Docks, with a water area of 93 hectares (230 acres), comprised the largest enclosed, impounded dock water in the world. On the south side of Royal Victoria Dock were four of Britain's largest flour mills. Royal Albert Dock had special cold stores for frozen meat, the largest capable of housing 250,000 carcases of mutton. Five hundred tonnes of timber could be accommodated at Surrey Commercial Docks. Tilbury Docks boasted 56 kilometres (35 miles) of railway sidings. Its passenger landing stage catered for massive liners, whatever the state of the tide. And such was the optimism of the 1960s that Tilbury Docks was given a £6 million face-lift, which involved constructing four new berths.

London's docklands helped to win the Second World War. Three thousand convoys sailed from here between 1939 and 1945. From the USA and Canada munitions were shipped and unloaded. D-Day saw more than two hundred merchant ships leave the docks for France, carrying stores, tanks, jeeps and ammunition. And between then and VE-Day some 2,750,000 tonnes of stores left this port to support the allied offensive.

Below: SS *Belgenland* moored at the North Quay of Royal Albert Dock in 1924, the largest vessel at that time to have sailed into the docks.

4 5

Hitler's Luftwaffe fought back savagely, with sustained nightly air attacks, for two months. When the war was over, the docks had suffered damage amounting to £13,500,000. During the Blitz the Port of London Authority lost one-third of its warehouses as well as half of its storage spaces. Yet the docks recovered. By 1959 the annual tonnage handled by the port

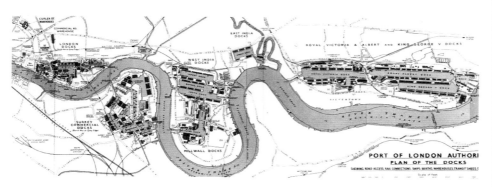

had risen from 40 million tonnes at the end of the war to more than 50 million tonnes.

By the early 1960s the port of London was annually handling yet more – over 65 million tonnes of cargo. In 1966 shipping arriving and departing from the port of London amounted to more than 91 million registered tonnes. Imports, exports and trans-shipments amounted to some 50 million tonnes. More than a hundred vessels a day were using the Royal Docks alone. The Port of London Authority even invested £1.3 million reconstructing the old western entrance to Royal Victoria Dock.

But new methods of handling cargoes began to spell the end of the old docklands. Shipyards built vessels too large for the old docks. Containerization was introduced, partly as a result of the Vietnam War, to enable huge amounts of material to be shipped in cargoes that were proof against pilfering. It was estimated by the Port of London Authority that 21 container berths could handle

everything previously catered for by 160 enclosed docks and 300 riverside wharves. Containerization meant that the bulk of the trade moved down the river to Tilbury, where more up-to-date facilities had been built.

Soon new roll-on-roll-off terminals had put up to 27,000 dockers out of work. At Tilbury around 50 million tonnes of merchandise a year could now be handled by a mere 3,000 dockers. More than 60 shipping companies were now operating from here, and soon some 100 passenger vessels were calling annually at Tilbury. As for container trucks, these too helped the decline of the old docklands, for they could scarcely operate in the narrow streets that led down to the old wharves and warehouses.

Above: A Port of London Authority map showing the docks as they were in 1960.

Right: The warehouses of Eastern Basin, St Katharine Docks, set aflame during the Blitz of 1940.

Below: The Victorian warehouses of Butlers Wharf have been transformed into apartments, shops, offices, workshops and restaurants.

So these historic docks began progressively to close down: East India Docks in 1967; St Katharine Docks in 1968; Millwall and West India Docks in 1978; the Royal Docks in 1981. Whereas in the 1950s the Watermen, Lightermen, Tugmen and Bargemen's Union boasted 5,500 members, by 1980 these numbered fewer than 200.

Always militant in the defence of their rights, the dockers used their traditional methods to fight containerization. In defiance of court orders, they began to picket container lorries. Three were threatened with prison sentences. In July 1972 five others were imprisoned in Pentonville gaol for blacking lorries at the Midland Cold Storage Company's terminal at Stratford. Now 170,000 dockers came out on strike, and the 'Pentonville five' were released after five days. But as the former trades unionist Lord Howie, writing on dock labour history in 1986, ironically observed, 'in opposing modernization, it is likely that the dockers' militancy was a factor in the decline and eventual death of London's docks.'

There were of course other reasons. More and more countries were successfully competing with Britain's traditional industries, particularly shipbuilding. Investment in road transport developed a new infrastructure in competition with the ships that had brought, for example, coals from Newcastle and other merchandise from yet further afield. Coal was also increasingly transported by rail, not by sea. Free trade and the abolition of restrictive port legislation made it easier for rival ports to compete with London.

Once it began, the docks' decline was rapid. A government report of 1962 (the Rochdale Report) had already recommended the closure of the London and St Katharine Docks and the development of Tilbury as an alternative. In the decade ending in the mid-1970s and before the closure of the Royal Docks, some 150,000 jobs were lost. Businesses disinvested, closed down or moved away. What had taken over 200 years to create disintegrated in just 14 years. Only 39,000 people lived in Docklands in 1981, a decline of 16,000 since 1976. Half of its land area was derelict.

Yet even in its heyday, London's docklands were in many respects an oddity, a backwater. As Peter Turlik, Director of Strategic Affairs for the LDDC, told an

international conference at Valencia in 1995, Docklands had been an area without coherence or stature. 'Historically and physically, the docks had been cut off from the mainstream of London life, hidden for centuries behind historic high brick walls and the area perceived as the backyard of London, overshadowed by the achievements of the adjacent City of London and neglected in the general tendency of cities, to spread westwards.'

Plans for regeneration were envisaged, publicly debated and repeatedly aborted. In January 1973 a study jointly sponsored by the Department of the Environment and the Greater London Council suggested various such schemes. The following year

Above left: **When King George V Dock opened on 8 July 1921 these cranes – altogether 42 of them, all built by Babcock and Wilcox – stretched 12.5 metres (42 feet) over the water.**

the Greater London Council and the London Boroughs of Tower Hamlets, Newham, Southwark, Lewisham and Greenwich set up the Docklands Joint Committee, charged with producing a strategic plan for the overall redevelopment of Docklands. The plan was published in 1976, its aim (expressed in a fine example of official jargon) being 'to use the

opportunity provided by large areas of London dockland becoming available for development to redress the housing, social, environmental, economic and communications deficiencies of the Docklands and parent boroughs and thereby to provide the freedom for similar improvements through east and inner London.'

From disrepair to regeneration: run-down (above) and restored warehouses (right) in Shad Thames, Butlers Wharf.

Few took up the challenge. Industries did not respond with new initiatives in the area. Indeed, one of the fundamental problems of this report was that it envisaged merely more of the past: warehousing, ship repairs, heavy engineering, the processing of raw food. The report also called for public investment of some £1.2 billion. It did not look to the private sector for major help in the way the LDDC did later.

Between the publication of the report and 1980 a further 8,500 or so jobs disappeared. In June of the following year a House of Lords Select Committee observed that considerable progress had been made in physically reclaiming Docklands, but added that a tremendous amount of development was still needed and that problems of attracting private investment had urgently to be overcome.

The following month the London Docklands Development Corporation was set up. In the light of previous failures to restore Docklands to life, the Secretary of State responsible, Michael Heseltine, perceived that 'London Docklands can only be successfully regenerated by a single-minded development agency.'

He also spelled out the magnitude of the task, declaring that London Docklands 'displays more acutely and extensively than any other area in England, the physical decline of the inner city and the need for urban area regeneration. It represents a major opportunity for the

development that London needs over the last twenty years of the twentieth century: new housing, new environment, new industrial development, new facilities for recreation, new commercial development, new architecture; all calculated to bring these barren areas back into more valuable use.' Michael Heseltine also recognized the scale of the investment required: 'This transformation from decline to renewal, from a problem area to an opportunity one, can only be achieved by a level of public expenditure that only the exchequer can afford.'

In Valencia Peter Turlik pointed out what had been seen as four potential assets of London Docklands. In the first place the area possessed space – it was, as he put it, 'the only major redevelopment area with land, which was capable of redressing many of the employment and economic deficiencies, of not only the Docklands itself, but also its surrounding areas.'

Secondly, London Docklands is close to the City and Central London, so that easy access could be obtained to the financial, commercial and other services of London. 'Its strategic location in the heart of the South East region, the most prosperous in the United Kingdom, and its proximity to the major markets of Continental Europe were also perceived as major advantages.'

Thirdly, the Isle of Dogs had been proposed as an Enterprise Zone (and was established as such in April 1982 with a life of ten years). The Isle of Dogs possessed enclosed dock water; it was close to the Thames; there was the possibility of renewed vitality and financial development.

Finally, Turlik declared that altogether 160 hectares (395 acres) of enclosed dock water, plus the River Thames itself, if properly utilized, provided a unique waterscape environment offering scope for leisure activities unrivalled not only in London but in the whole South East region of Britain. A powerful body was needed to capitalize on all these assets.

So Michael Heseltine's 'single-minded development agency' was set up, and for the most part it triumphed. This was to be an unelected body, responsible simply to central government. Each of its board members was appointed by the Secretary of State for the Environment for a period of three years, with places on the board reserved for individuals nominated by the three municipal authorities.

Reg Ward, formerly shadow Chief Executive of the LDDC, now stepped into the role for real. Under his impetus, the LDDC addressed several problems to transform Docklands. The most urgent was the provision of an adequate, virtually new transport system. First, a series of red-brick roads were built to improve

Above: West India and Millwall Docks before their transformation. *Right:* The River Thames winds around the new, revitalized West India Docks. Behind are the Surrey Docks peninsula and the City of London.

Reg Ward had been canny in recruiting Peter Turlik, formerly a planner with the Greater London Council. Turlik had been involved with the GLC from 1968, working on redevelopment proposals for St Katharine Docks. Three years later he had joined a small, multi-disciplinary group working with consultancy engineers Travers Morgan, who were prospecting

space,' he recalls. In August, September and October 1980 he walked around Docklands. Coming across pieces of railway track, he mused, 'What about a new railway?' There was existing track already, part of it elevated. In November of that year he was in Minneapolis, where his picture of the elevated railway took shape. He flew home by way of Toronto, to view that city's transport system, and was confirmed in his view that a light railway in London's Docklands was perfectly feasible and might cost around £64 million. This was at a time when only about 40,000 people lived in Docklands. But such a railway would attract many more jobs.

Reg Ward chartered a helicopter to enthuse Michael Heseltine, tracing for him from above the possible route of a light railway. He gained outline approval for what is now the Docklands Light Railway.

Ward believed in breaking conventional rules. He believed that random initiatives paid off in a job whose prospects were totally unpredictable. One project that came about in this way was London City Airport. In September 1981 Ward was

accessibility within and around the Enterprise Zone on the Isle of Dogs. Next came the Docklands Clipper, a shuttle bus which ran between Mile End tube station and the Isle of Dogs. Set up in January 1984, it closed down five years later, when the Docklands Light Railway was making it increasingly redundant. But by that time the service was providing clippers at five-minute intervals and carrying some 12,000 passengers a week.

Left: Shadwell Basin today. This masterly piece of industrial architecture, completed in 1858, now boasts a watersports centre. The spire of St Paul's Church is just visible.

Above: Shadwell Basin in 1985, before its regeneration.

early options for redeveloping Docklands. After another three years he was seconded to the Docklands Joint Committee to work on the development of the London Docklands Strategic Plan.

Reg Ward persuaded Peter Turlik to resign from the GLC in the year before the LDDC moved into action. They worked together on the land vesting programme, before Peter Turlik was commissioned to help set up and for three years promote the Isle of Dogs Enterprise Zone.

The task of regenerating Docklands still seemed to require miracles. But miracles occurred, stimulated by Reg Ward's serendipity. Ward wasted no time in using the 'fallow year' before the LDDC officially came into being. 'I had a year of free were pre-sold. The builders asked for more land, and Beckton gradually developed into one of the strongest housing programmes in London. The Chief Executive's powers of persuasion were formidable. By the end of 1983 he had even cajoled a telephone company to put a fibre-optic ring main around Docklands at a time when there was no one to use it.

invited to lunch by Philip Beck, the Chairman of Mowlem Engineers and Construction. Initially he supposed he might discuss what might happen in Wapping and the Isle of Dogs. But the conversation turned to the Royal Docks – isolated, partly cut off by marshlands. On this occasion Ward also met Bill Brymon, who operated out of Plymouth airport a 50-seater turbo-prop plane known as the Dash 7.

A week before Christmas a plan was ready to fly such planes out of a new airport beside the Royal Docks. 'All hell broke loose,' says Reg Ward. 'We were hammered from all sides.' So he took a dozen local people to Plymouth to see the Dash 7 in operation. They found it acceptable. Some members of the LDDC board were horrified, but the momentum had been created. A public enquiry of 1985 agreed that London City Airport should be built. Its first two operators were Brymon Airways (which was closely allied to British Airways) and a subsidiary of British Midland called Eurocity Express.

There were other remarkable achievements under Reg Ward's stewardship of London Docklands. Addressing the House Building Federation in May 1981, he found builders (Barratt, Wimpey, Broseley and Comben) who responded positively to the notion of creating new houses in Docklands, entirely at risk, offering them a 12-hectare (30-acre) site at Beckton. All the houses

Ward also deliberately planned a dramatic change in the face of Docklands. Development in old buildings would have meant an attempt to recreate the past. Far better, in Ward's view, was to stimulate smaller, modern development – such as Skylines and Heron Quays. Nearly 186,000 square metres (two million square feet) of property on the Isle of Dogs was demolished to prevent it being reused. A new spirit was enthusing London's Docklands – moreover one that brooked no interference from the stagnant ideas that had brought the region to its present plight. Speaking of those who wanted to curb his flair, Ward said, 'One listened, debated and then went ahead.'

In the early years the Department of Environment funded the new LDDC annually with grants of between £60 million and £70 million. By 1990 this figure had exceeded £300 million. These seemingly colossal amounts of money were in fact far from adequate for the yet more colossal task ahead. As part

of its operating philosophy, the LDDC determined that its own financial resources should be used to attract private investment in Docklands.

This was a remarkably successful policy. By 1997 the LDDC had managed to find private investors willing to put more than £6.505 billion into Docklands. British newspapers, including 75 per cent of London-printed national dailies, had been persuaded to transfer from Fleet Street, with the *Telegraph* also building printworks on Millwall Dock on the Isle of Dogs, and News International, publishers of *The Times* and the *Sun* at Wapping. the *Guardian* and the *Financial Times* also built printworks in the area. In 1996 *Reader's Digest* decided to move from Berkeley Square to Westferry Circus at Canary Wharf.

Above left: **Vital for the new image of Docklands was the transfer from Fleet Street of the premises of major national newspapers, such as the *Daily Telegraph*, whose newsroom is pictured here.**

Right: **Beckton has been transformed by developers, as this attractive housing complex at Winsor Park clearly shows.**

By this time nearly 2,400 new companies had set up business in Docklands. British Gas invested in a new ring main on the Isle of Dogs in 1982, when the future use of the facility was far from certain. A TV and film studio was set up in the same locality. An enterprise centre was set up in Southwark, boosted by £1.5 million from the LDDC, with 46 workspaces let at extremely low initial rates for start-up business.

By 1997 more than 72,000 people worked in Docklands, against the 1981 figure of 27,200. People had moved in, swelling the population from 39,400 to 80,000. To house them, more than 21,600 homes had been built, many of them owner-occupied – some 43 per cent, compared with the 5 per cent of the population owning homes in 1981.

Job opportunities were no longer primarily those of watermen, lightermen or dock labourers. So the LDDC put some of its resources into training facilities, sponsoring initially over 5,000 training places in a remarkable range of occupational skills. Once again, help was sought from the private sector. British Telecom and the supermarket chain Tesco

supported schemes to train their future staff. Companies such as John Mowlem and J. Jarvis & Sons, as well as Olympia & York, who built Canary Wharf, co-operated in setting up training schemes for future construction and office workers.

In 1990–91 alone the LDDC contributed more than £14 million to 64 different educational and training projects, teaching over 4,500 people. In Surrey Docks building began on Bacon's City Technology College, with a grant from the Corporation of more than £3 million. Some £10 million was contributed to the new

building for the Tower Hamlets College in Poplar, designed for the training of the over-16s. And for £1 million the Corporation bought 480 computers for 33 Docklands schools – giving this area the highest computer–pupil ratio in the whole of Britain.

In Bermondsey Riverside alone the LDDC disbursed £75,000 to St Joseph's Roman Catholic Primary School, £34,000 to St Michael's Roman Catholic Secondary School and £35,000 to the Riverside Primary School. The Corporation's final commitment, before handing back Bermondsey Riverside to the local authority, was £263,000 to Butlers Wharf Chef School, a project set up in partnership with the London Borough of Southwark, Conran Restaurants and the Hotel and Catering Company.

Above: **Two examples of the modern thrust of London Docklands: Tower Hamlets College and BT's satellite earth station in Silvertown.** *Right:* **Alfred Salter Primary School, Surrey Docks.**

Traditional industries that had remained in Docklands had expanded, supported by the LDDC. In his Chairman's statement in 1996, Sir Michael noted that 'Europe's largest cane sugar refiners, Tate & Lyle, whose predecessor first opened for business here in 1878, invested some £20 million on improvements during the year, and will be investing a further £90 million

Sir Terence Conran's involvement in this educational project was natural. Bermondsey's riverfront has a complex of four restaurants and five specialist food shops, all owned by Conran Restaurants. He himself recalled that some of his earliest memories involve London's docklands. 'As a small boy, I was sometimes brought here by my father, a dealer in gum copal resin with an office in Stepney,' he wrote. 'Together, we would come down to Docklands and watch freighters from the Belgian Congo unloading their cargoes.' He also witnessed Docklands' decline, what he described as 'neglect and dereliction', and then 'the area's renaissance as a vibrant part of London, a process that is still under way'.

In 1997, the year before the LDDC closed down, its Chairman Sir Michael Pickard rejoiced in this educational expansion. In 1981, he reflected, 75 per cent of Docklands' pupils left school at the earliest opportunity. By 1997 75 per cent were staying on for higher education.

over the next three years'; meanwhile, he reported, 'Pura Foods, one of Europe's largest edible oil manufacturers, announced a programme to expand their already substantial presence near the mouth of the River Lea.'

To achieve all this the LDDC was not only substantially funded; it was also given remarkable, indeed controversial powers. First, special parliamentary vesting procedures enabled the Corporation to acquire land from public sector authorities. Following its declared policy of attracting private investment, it was

decided that as much public land as possible, given the financial constraints on the Corporation, should be bought, and once reclamation and servicing had been carried out by the LDDC, this should be resold to the private sector for new development.

Above: **Riverside walkways, many of them offering stunning views as here at Butlers Wharf, are a major feature of London Docklands.**
Right: **At Plaistow Wharf, Silvertown, Tate and Lyle continue their long-established sugar trade.**

Secondly, in April 1982 the government declared the area around the former docks on the Isle of Dogs an Enterprise Zone, a designation which would last ten years, and the LDDC was made the Enterprise Zone authority. The zone offered tax allowances to both investors and developers. Thirdly, the LDDC replaced the three local authorities of Newham, Southwark and Tower Hamlets as the planning authority for the area and soon established a reputation for providing a speedy and responsive planning service to developers and investors.

Initial decisions were not always successful. A critical observer, Stephanie Williams, in her Phaidon architectural guide to Docklands, spotted what had happened after the LDDC, in the spring of 1982, offered to anybody wanting to build industrial or commercial buildings in the Enterprise Zone centred on Millwall Dock, West India Docks and East India Dock the Enterprise Zone's allowance of 'freedom from planning restrictions, exemption from rates and 100 per cent tax relief for the next ten years'. Absurdly coloured, unrelated sheds and simple buildings rose in a sea of mud and wasteland. But, she added, with no strategic plan, a couple of hundred staff and a conscious hands-off approach, the LDDC had succeeded in turning popular perception of Docklands from a wasteland of near dereliction to a boom town of what she dubbed 'over-heated development'. Today not everyone agrees with this harsh judgement.

To attract new residents to London's depleted Docklands, improvements were

Right: **The LDDC has pioneered new bridges, walkways and homes, while preserving the older features of this architecturally precious part of London.**

needed in the quality of housing, as well as transport, schools and other amenities in the area. Once again, the LDDC's plan was to attempt to promote all this not solely by its own resources but in partnership with the private sector, which would recognize the value of a regenerated part of London.

And there was one major oddity in the Corporation's remit. The LDDC was deliberately prevented from making statutory plans. Such powers were retained by the local authorities. The LDDC was meant to be flexible, responding to the needs of developers, taking drastic action instead of sitting back. Its Director of Strategic Affairs, Peter Turlik, described the approach as it applied to the Isle of Dogs. 'Instead of a rigid land plan, most forms of commercial use were automatically allowed to proceed, subject to health and safety regulations,' he wrote. 'Once a major user or occupier was attracted to a specific site, that became a land use fix determining the nature of adjacent developments, which, in an organic manner, were allowed to grow around it.'

Another vital decision in the early years was to halt the process of filling in the enclosed docks. Instead of seeing these closed docks as a problem, the LDDC rightly decided that they were assets. Dwellings overlooking water are prized. Historic warehouses could be transformed into flats. The property market was at last, once again, interested in London Docklands.

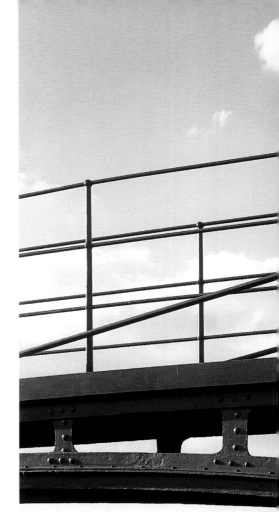

Docklands, with the World Trade Centre development at St Katharine-by-the-Tower, the historic attractions of Wapping and the former docks in the Isle of Dogs, will create a new route between the Tower, Tower Bridge and Greenwich.'

The first campaign that promoted Docklands had as its symbol a crow,

There remained the task of promoting and marketing Docklands. In spite of all that was being achieved, the old, dilapidated, derelict image remained. As Chairman Nigel Broackes put it in 1983, the regeneration of Docklands was then very much a matter of faith as well as action. 'It is not merely a question of reassuring those already in the area whose hopes have been somewhat tarnished by years of pervasive economic decline,' he said. 'The world outside has to be convinced that change is really imminent and that investment will reap its due success.' He added that one of London's most important industries is tourism, not only in terms of jobs but also of financial turnover. The Chairman declared that 'there is every reason to hope that

Left: Cranes rise above Canary Wharf, under construction. The development became a potent symbol of Docklands' new vision and regeneration.
Above right: Converted warehouses flank the Thames at Limehouse, perfect examples of how the area's redundant buildings have been put to new use.

perched on top of Nelson's column in Trafalgar Square. Looking east, the crow said, 'Why move to the middle of nowhere when you can move to the middle of London?' (The middle of nowhere apparently included such aggressively marketed places as Milton Keynes.) Then promotion stopped, for the mid-1980s were boom years for Docklands.

Arguably the building of Canary Wharf was instrumental in the upturn in Docklands' fortunes. In 1985 rising rentals and the shortage of suitable buildings in the City led three American banks to propose the creation of a 1.1 million square metre (12.2 million square foot) business development of offices, shops, restaurants, public spaces and conference facilities

through their adviser G. Ware Travelstead. The centrepiece of the development was to be an immense 50-storey tower, the tallest in the UK, which would make Docklands the site of a new London landmark.

At the eleventh hour, G. Ware Travelstead was unable to secure funding for the scheme, and it was taken over by Olympia & York, one of the largest North American property developers, under the ownership of Paul Reichmann. The master building agreement between the LDDC and Olympia & York was finally signed in July 1987, and construction began.

Paul Reichmann came from one of the ten richest families in the world. Their assets amounted to £10 billion. He once told an ally, 'It was God's will that I was successful on such a scale.' In the late 1980s Olympia & York's assets amounted to $25 billion. A devout Jew, Reichmann would not allow anyone to work on any of his projects (including Canary Wharf) on the Sabbath day. But the Canary Wharf tower, and another ten buildings, were completed by 1991, at a cost of $3 billion, and 55 per cent of them were let. To quote Professor S. K. Al Naib, head of the department of civil engineering at the University of East London, here Olympia & York 'created a "total environment", a whole new piece of a city. Westferry Circus is a large tree-ringed circus surrounded by buildings, with one segment open to the waterfront. It is the size of St James's Square and has been beautifully furnished with lamps, railings and benches. A tree-lined avenue leads into the first square, Cabot Square, which has an inner ring of trees around it and at the far side a glass-roofed retail building full of shops and restaurants, and beyond is the dome of the Docklands Light Railway Station and the giant 50-storey tower. The public garden is surrounded by silver lime trees and has the tallest fountain in London.'

A promoter's nightmare then occurred. On Black Monday, 1992, the stock markets crashed and Reichmann's empire crashed with them. He fought hard to save it. One historian (Anthony Bianco) has gone so far as to say of Reichmann: 'He was trying to present greater financial resources than existed in the belief that he would pull it off, that he could save O & Y.' However, Reichmann failed, and saw his wealth reduced to a mere £100 million. He gave up control of Olympia & York Canary Wharf Ltd London to administrators. In Toronto he filed for bankruptcy protection. But the consequences were even more wide-ranging: with the collapse of Canary

Wharf, people and businesses began to think twice about moving into Docklands. The proposed Jubilee Line Extension linking the Isle of Dogs to the West End via London Bridge, which was to have been funded with a contribution from Olympia & York, foundered.

Left: Texaco's headquarters at Canary Wharf indicate that, once again, London Docklands is thriving.
Right: Cabot Square, Canary Wharf. The buildings are spectacular, the gushing fountain entrancing, and the constant throng of people proof of how much this newly created environment is enjoyed.

Below: Limehouse Basin today. The dock was originally constructed to join up the Grand Union Canal at Paddington with London's docks.

Opposite: Limehouse Basin in the early 1980s, before its restoration. In the background is the lovely church of St Anne, which Nicholas Hawksmoor designed in the late 1720s.

As she points out, a high-quality environment contributes to the quality of people's lives. So the LDDC has helped by planting more than 160,000 trees and landscaping 222 hectares (549 acres) of land. Other treats (among some hundred annual events sponsored by the LDDC to promote Docklands) are an annual Seafood Festival, the Greenwich + Docklands

Eventually the nightmare came to an end. In November 1993 the banks re-financed Canary Wharf, and International Property Corporation Ltd – a group of property developers including Paul Reichmann – were able to buy it back at the end of 1995. Paul Reichmann was appointed manager, with a 5 per cent share. By 1997 over 80 per cent of Canary Wharf was let, and work was being finalized on the extension of the Jubilee Line.

The 1995 sale of Canary Wharf to International Property Corporation Ltd was the biggest property deal ever done in Europe. As LDDC Chairman Sir Michael Pickard observed, 'It made headlines in every important newspaper in the world, and dramatized the coming of age of London Docklands as a business district of global importance.' But it had been a close-run thing...

At a time when the residential population had grown from its low of 40,000 to 80,000, Sunny Crouch, Marketing and Public Affairs Director of the LDDC, emphasized her belief that 'the key to long-term success will be how the area feels for people, whether living in, working in, or visiting the area.' In 1993 these visitors numbered 1.2 million, rising to 1.6 million in 1995.

International Festival and the sponsoring by the LDDC of the Docklands Sinfonietta, which eventually received direct Arts Council funding and renamed itself Sinfonia 21.

'The task of regeneration in London Docklands has been an all-embracing one,' declared Sunny Crouch. 'Much of the effort and much of the spend has been dedicated to achieving physical regeneration with the establishment of an entirely new transport infrastructure, new commercial and industrial space and new homes.' She also notes: 'The enduring feature which brings quality of life to the area for its residents, its workers and its visitors is the provision for leisure.'

Tourism creates jobs for Docklands. In 1995 tourists spent £8.6 million in the

area. Attracting visitors encourages both investment and development, one of the major aims of the LDDC. Butlers Wharf in Southwark, for example, now boasts restaurants (employing 500 people), art galleries, two museums and many shops, all opened since 1985. And of course the area benefits from the glamour of the Tower and Tower Bridge, which, along with Tower Bridge Museum and HMS *Belfast*, attract nearly two and a half million visitors each year.

Increasingly perceived by the general public as a tourist area, in 1993 the Docklands region attracted 360,000 tourists to St Katharine Docks, 350,000 to Canary Wharf, 240,000 to the Design Museum, 220,000 to Island Gardens, 160,000 to Butlers Wharf and to Hay's Galleria, 110,000 to HMS *Belfast* and riverside pubs.

Existing restaurants and pubs in Docklands began to flourish again, while new eating-places sprouted. Canary Wharf soon attracted them: MPW (founded by Marco Pierre White), the Seattle Coffee Company, the Gourmet Pizza Company, Café Rouge and inevitably an Italian restaurant called Amerigo Vespucci. Café Rouge also makes another appearance in Hay's Galleria.

In 1860, in *The Uncommercial Traveller*, Charles Dickens memorably described the dockland fare of yester-year. 'Down by the Docks,' he wrote, 'you may buy polonies, saveloys, and sausage preparations various, if you are not particular what they are made of besides seasoning.' In his time oysters were cheap – so cheap in

Concerts, exhibitions and conferences now take place in Cabot Hall at Canary Wharf. To promote all these activities the LDDC set up a visitor centre on the Isle of Dogs. Each year up to 170,000 people have used it, 34 per cent of them from overseas.

Limehouse Basin also attracts visitors and tourists.The LDDC co-operated with the British Waterways Board to restore the marina moorings. Narrowboat rallies drew more attention to its pleasures, and beginning in the summer of 1994 this became the site of a Limehouse festival.

Hay's Galleria is a perfect example of what can be accomplished in Docklands after disasters. The first was the great fire of Tooley Street in 1861, which meant that the warehouses built only six years earlier to store wines, spirits and groceries had to be rebuilt. The second disaster was the Blitz, which again demolished parts of these warehouses. Now their waterfronts have been reconstructed to their original Victorian form. Inside are shops, offices, apartments and maisonettes. The glazed Galleria itself, built in 1986 on the twisting site of what was once Hay's Dock, rises on welded steel columns and embodies restaurants, a pub, specialist shops and a public meeting-place.

Above: The sturdy warehouses of Hay's Dock were designed by W. Snooke and H. Stock in the mid-1850s and rebuilt after the 1861 Tooley Street fire.
Right: Hay's Galleria, built on the site of Hay's Dock, is popular with both locals and visitors. One of its many attractive features is its curved roof.

fact that they often filled out meat dishes. Dockers' family celebrations were usually accompanied by meals of whitebait. Jellied eels were a favoured dockland dish. And before the end of the nineteenth century the Chinese had already arrived in the East End, bringing their own distinctive restaurants and food.

Today, as in Canary Wharf, some of these new restaurant openings have attractive foreign names, reflecting the international aspect of this newly revived part of London. Le Pont de la Tour, for example, opened in 1991 at Butlers Wharf, and in the same location the following year appeared the Cantina del Ponte. Captain Tony's Pizza and Pasta graced Tower Piazza in the same year. Subsequently arrived the Lotus Chinese Floating Restaurant (Britain's largest floating restaurant), Pizzeria La Lanterna, the Bengal Clipper, Harry's Bar at Glengall Bridge and El Pirata Tapas Bar. Possibly Tooley Street, with Le Truffe Noir and the High Note Jazz Bar, deserves the accolade for the most incongruous mix of names.

Soon some of their chefs were winning awards. The chef of Thamesview, at 66–67 Amsterdam Road on the Isle of Dogs, was voted National Curry Chef of the year in 1996. Lancer Brasserie, flourishing in an old pub at Westferry Road, gained its prize as the Best Indian Restaurant at the London Docklands Good Food Awards of 1996. And the long-established Chinese tradition still exists in Docklands. The Tai Pan Chinese Restaurant, at 665 Commercial Road, was runner-up for the Best Oriental Restaurant award of the same year.

Perry's Dock, in Clove Crescent, close by Billingsgate Market, naturally specializes in fish dishes. An Italian restaurant, Fino's Orangery, at Harbour Exchange on the Isle of Dogs, also specializes in fish dishes and in 1996 was judged Business Restaurant of the Year in the same competition. For those who prefer British cooking, the exquisite Dockmaster's House at West India Dock Gate, Hertsmere Road, is an ideal setting.

The four-star Scandic Crown Hotel (now called the Holiday Inn Nelson Dock) opened in 1991 with 390 beds. One of its conference centres is housed in a handsome Grade II listed building, Nelson House, which was built in 1740 for a rich shipbuilder. Another imaginative touch was to tow a replica of a French sailing barge from Southampton and winch it into the dry dock to serve as the hotel's gourmet seafood restaurant.

Right: **Dickens Inn, one of Docklands' enchanting waterside pubs. First built in the 1790s, it was moved to its present site in 1974. Its bars bear the names of some of Dickens's best-known characters.**

Below: Holiday Inn
Nelson Dock,
completed in 1991,
is home to a replica
of a French sailing
barge.

Other hotels followed as the region began to prosper. By July 1997 five more new hotels were scheduled for Docklands. Budget chain Ibis had agreed an 88-bedroom hotel on the Isle of Dogs; Granada was building a 132-bedroom hotel on the A13 at East India Dock; a 220-bedroom hotel was planned at West India Quay; another 150-bedroom riverside hotel was under construction at Canary Wharf; and a 258-bedroom hotel had been designed to occupy never-completed offices at South Quay Waterside.

Not far away from the Holiday Inn rises the Rotherhithe Youth Hostel, which also opened in 1991 with facilities for 320 beds, a cafeteria and a conference room. And beside the Holiday Inn is an 1868 engine house, whose hydraulic lift once raised ships out of the water for repair at Nelson Dock – which survived as London's only dry dock until the 1960s. Close by is the Blacksmith's Arms, its name mirrored in its horseshoe-shaped bar. Ask the bartenders to show you the brass plaque which indicates the flood level of January 1928 (long before the construction of the Thames Barrier), when every house along this riverside was inundated.

In 1991 Michael Heseltine, who had set up the LDDC ten years previously, could be well pleased. 'The legacy of the LDDC,' he said, 'will be new buildings, new infrastructures, new skills and new hope. They have killed the myth that East London has no future.' Many of Docklands' citizens (though not quite all of them) were equally well pleased. Others in the LDDC sang their own praises, and rightly. Said former LDDC Chairman Sir David Hardy, 'Working in partnership with private developers, the three local boroughs of Tower Hamlets, Newham and Southwark and many other statutory authorities, the balance of London is being shifted to the East.' Eric Sorensen as Chief Executive gave a vision of the future: 'The overall measure of success as we complete the LDDC's remit will be to engender a sense of civic pride in the area and ensure that London Docklands plays a full part in the larger, thriving capital city.'

Above: **The Grapes in Limehouse, thought to be the inspiration for The Six Jolly Fellowship Porters in Dickens's *Our Mutual Friend*; a hostelry designed 'to soften the human breast'.**

Differing Visions and Tangled Politics

3

Hell hath no fury like a woman spurned.

William Shakespeare

Opposite: **When it lost its role as the capital's main port, Docklands became isolated from the rest of the city.**

There were three women spurned when the London Docklands Development Corporation was set up in 1981: the local authorities of Newham, Southwark and Tower Hamlets.

One can hear their anger in many writings of the time. 'Anyone who regards as a success story the systematic attacks by the LDDC on local and strategic planning, and on local accountability, the confiscation of practically all the housing land in the Dockland part of Newham, Southwark and Tower Hamlets, the loss of thousands of jobs traditional to the area, the madcap schemes for an airport, luxury housing, and huge office developments, cannot be said to have the interests of Docklands at heart,' wrote George Nicholson in 1986. 'The truth is that Docklands is up for sale to the highest bidder. A great opportunity for Londoners has been lost.'

George Nicholson, once a seaman and ships' engineer, was elected to Southwark Council to represent a riverside ward. In 1981 he was elected to represent Bermondsey on the Greater London Council. In his own words, he later found himself 'locked in a battle with another ex-seaman', Sir Christopher Benson, the then Chairman of the LDDC. As a democratically elected councillor, he deeply resented the remedy imposed by the government on London's declining Docklands, the creation of a democratically-unaccountable authority,

Left: A community undergoing transformation: work progresses on Westferry Road, Isle of Dogs, in the late 1980s.

which in his view was 'the beginning of a process which we are now seeing driven to a bitter conclusion, with the capital city itself plunged back into its mid-nineteenth-century condition, fragmented, controlled not by a unified elected government but by a muddle of quangos and joint boards.'

Some planners and architects disagreed with the attempt to regenerate the area without an overall master plan to guide development. Peter Turlik, the LDDC's Director of Strategic Affairs, argues that London Docklands was never a greenfield site. 'It was part of the Inner City, and therefore it already had an urban framework – neglected yes, but in place.' It had an existing population, with inadequate facilities, including poor road and transport links. Nevertheless, 'all these elements provided a "skeleton framework" which needed to be fleshed out, a skeleton which did not need to be thrown out, but rather seen as an asset to be nurtured, and slowly brought back to life.'

These elements scarcely did this. The population was only 39,000; jobs were hard to find; new schools were needed; and Docklands had an extremely sad image. Furthermore, the LDDC was charged with kick-starting regeneration without having first developed a strategic plan. Peter Turlik resolutely defends the government's thinking. Ministers wanted the Corporation to be 'flexible and responsive to the needs of the

Below: Not everyone approved of the LDDC's regeneration plans, as this demonstration depicting the 'death of a community' clearly shows.

development industry, with a desire to see an early implementation of schemes, rather than the Corporation spending its first years in plan formulation.' The government believed that the region needed 'some early immediate and urgent action'. Virtually the sole exception to this was to safeguard infrastructure and service corridors.

Reg Ward, the LDDC's first Chief Executive, is even blunter in response to the criticism that a master plan should have been set out. 'I have a difficulty with that,' he avers. 'It presumes you know what can be attracted to an area; but you can't.' The paradox involved is this: to attract investment in infrastructure, business and housing, it is necessary to show the demand for it; but in the early years of regenerating such a run-down area, such a demand cannot be demonstrated, since up until then it does not exist. Hence Reg Ward's own remarkable approach to regenerating Docklands – one that broke conventional rules and was, in his own words, 'irrational, hopeful, enthusiastic and lucky'. In the end his approach succeeded.

He describes the creation of Canary Wharf, the highly-visible centrepiece of London's Docklands, as 'the biggest accident of all'. Initially, two celebrated chefs and restaurateurs, the Roux brothers, needed a 372 square-metre (4,000 square-foot) shed. Reg Ward leased a Thames barge, which was used as a restaurant, moored near a shed on Canary Wharf. The chairman of the American bank funding the project was inspired to take up this shed as a back-up office. Next the firm

decided to establish larger offices, asking for a six months' option on Canary Wharf. The board of the LDDC agreed. And suddenly Canary Wharf came splendidly alive.

'Suddenly,' says Reg Ward, 'it was easy to attract to Docklands development of quality.' One major development was that nearly all of the UK's newspapers moved offices and/or printworks to the area – newspapers that included *The Times*, the *Sunday Times*, the *Guardian*, the *Telegraph* group, the *Financial Times*, the *Daily Mirror* and the *Independent*. By 1991 75 per cent of all London-printed national daily newspapers were produced in London Docklands. Docklands was now London's Fleet Street.

In the meantime, by 1987 land prices had increased five-fold in fewer than 18 months. Canary Wharf, in the then Chief Executive's words, had created a 'bow-wave of momentum'. The momentum moved east from the Isle of Dogs and west back to the City of London.

Yet in promoting Canary Wharf, Reg Ward had consulted neither the Department of the Environment nor the local authorities. 'The whole of Canary Wharf,' Newham MP

Nigel Spearing wryly observed, 'needed less planning scrutiny than a change of use from a newsagent's to a fish-and-chip shop on the Commercial Road.'

Without the slightest doubt George Nicholson was right about the undemocratic nature of the LDDC. Personally appointed for three years or so by the Secretary of State for the Environment, its members were directly responsible not to any electors but to that same Secretary of State. Three places were retained for representatives of the three Docklands boroughs. The rest of the members were drawn almost entirely from the worlds of finance and business. The local communities felt they had little role in a body vital for their future.

George Nicholson was also right to add that, 'Historians of the future will study and judge the events of this extraordinary time.' Just over a decade later the historical consensus seems to be that the LDDC was for the most part an enormous success story. And it was a grave mistake for the members of the local community to decline on occasion the invitation to bring their unique knowledge of their localities to the service of the Corporation.

Right: **Regeneration proceeds apace: the view west from Manchester Road, Isle of Dogs, in 1989.**

In the first instance all three local authorities nominated their leaders to sit on the board of the LDDC. Southwark relinquished its seat at the end of 1984 and did not take it up again until the end of 1991; Newham chose not to be represented from May 1986 to May 1991; Tower Hamlets also gave up their seat in May 1986, but after a brief period, and with the election of a Liberal Democrat administration in the same year, nominated one of its councillors to the board.

Yet few could blame the three local authorities for initially resenting the cuckoo that had thrown them out of several of their nests. Here was a body with extensive powers and far more government money than they themselves could deploy. This new body had stripped powers from the local authorities, which it had now replaced as the single development control authority. It had been granted powers to acquire land speedily from the public sector authorities through special parliamentary procedures. It was in charge of the Isle of Dogs Enterprise Zone where businesses were now to be exempt from local authority taxes, planning permission was relaxed and both investors and developers were offered tax allowances.

What's more, this quango had been set up by Margaret Thatcher's Conservative government, while the three local councils were decidedly Labourite, with some councillors being on what was described as the far left. The pugnaciously entertaining Reg Ward, LDDC's first Chief Executive, decided that the best strategy would be for the most part to listen, to compromise, but if necessary simply to ignore the local authorities' complaints.

Another reason for the local authorities' non-co-operation with the LDDC was that the Labour party, it seemed, might soon be back in power and the balance of political strength in London Docklands might then change. In fact Labour lost the 1983 election, and continued to lose elections. The supposedly Conservative quango was clearly here to stay – at least until May 1997.

With hindsight, it would perhaps have been wiser if the LDDC had not occasionally rubbished those responsible for Docklands before 1981. One LDDC publication robustly (but rightly) observed that this was 'a period of much study, planning and research', adding that 'conversely it was a time of little effective action, to counter the drift into decline of population, employment and investment'.

Again, when Reg Ward resigned as Chief Executive at the end of 1987 he proclaimed that what had been achieved under his management was 'a far cry from the dereliction and despair which existed in 1980'. Though he was undoubtedly right, this could be construed as a smack in the face for those who had attempted to cope with the Docklands with far fewer resources than he and his team had been able to deploy.

Yet Reg Ward's description was nothing but the truth. In 1980 Docklands was largely derelict. This was not an area in

which the property market and its planners were remotely interested. The local authorities for the most part wished to fill in the docks for social housing. A mere 5 per cent or so of houses were owner-occupied. Residents were no doubt proud of their heritage, but they were also trapped – socially and physically. People in Wapping, for example, had scarcely any

Left: A 1982 shot of Butlers Wharf, Shad Thames, prior to its rebirth as a thriving complex of shops and restaurants.
Right: An inhabitant of Manchester Road, Isle of Dogs, resolutely keeps her street clean, even while her corner of Docklands is being radically transformed.

connection with people living on the Isle of Dogs. Those living in Silvertown rarely travelled to other parts of Docklands, let alone to the rest of London.

Small wonder that some of those devoting themselves to local politics at that time believed that the leaders of the LDDC were inclined to patronize them. It is an enormous tribute to both the executives

Below: A scene from
the past: Prestons
Road, Isle of Dogs,
c. 1982.

and staff of the councils and the Corporation that relations between these rival authorities were nonetheless built up, as well as those between the Corporation and others who were inclined initially to be hostile. One community activist, Ted Johns, was Chair of the Association of Island Communities. Reg Ward recollects fighting with such activists but also recalls that he and they respected each other. Ted Johns, for example, for the most part did not agree with the Chief Executive's plans, but did acknowledge that something, at last, was happening in Docklands.

As for the three local authorities, Reg Ward declares that, 'Theoretically they could have stopped us in our tracks.' They did not, in part because he went ahead quickly and comprehensively, producing results which not one of them would have wanted to claw back. Ostensibly, relations seemed impossible, but at the end of the day, once the local authorities and community activists learned what the Corporation was planning to do, even though some might object, they recognized that the LDDC could achieve much that the local councillors could not.

Undoubtedly the Corporation recognized the need to inform local people, setting up its own newspaper, *Docklands News*, which for the most part was published monthly and distributed door-to-door to businesses and residents throughout the area.

However, lack of co-operation did damage Docklands, as forewarned by the LDDC's Chairman Nigel (later Sir Nigel) Broackes in his 1983 report: 'Any lack of action,

support for or encouragement of the growing programme of improvement, investment and increasing opportunities in housing and jobs only means that the people of Docklands lose out.' He added, 'In this respect the London Borough of Southwark's continuing reluctance to work with the Corporation in the interests of local residents is much regretted.' He also insisted that, 'Despite occasional local political difficulties, the LDDC is forging ahead with the job set by Parliament. There is sufficient activity on the ground now to demonstrate that the very real problems in the area can be solved and that an urban development corporation

provides the right mix of will, enthusiasm, money and power to bring about change.'

The GLC was also at odds with the LDDC in some respects, sporadically attacking the Corporation and its actions. In 1983, the former LDDC Vice-Chairman and Labour MP Bob Mellish fulminated that an onslaught on the LDDC was 'an emotional attack from a discredited and dying body, which simply resents our success after its own failure to produce results'.

Bob Mellish insisted that, 'Far from betraying the people of Docklands, the Corporation is, together with the private sector, providing hope and change in the form of new homes, new jobs and a much better environment.' The pugnacious Reg Ward added, 'As the organization basically in charge of change, we expect to take a good deal of flak.'

Some years later, former members of the GLC might well be incensed by a judgement by Peter Turlik, Director of Strategic Affairs for the LDDC, that the 'socio-political' re-development plans prepared for the area in the 1970s by the Labour-controlled Greater London Council 'compounded the very reason why the area was declining, for the plans and the expectation they gave rise to were totally detached from the fundamental economic and technological changes taking place, not only in world shipping, but also in the world of business, finance and investment.' He added: 'As a result, an almost complete economic void existed, which had to be filled by activity, independent of, and other than, port-related functions.'

Michael Honey, Reg Ward's successor as Chief Executive of the LDDC, took on a remit to make friends with the local authorities (by this time the GLC had been abolished) and to improve relations with its local communities. The LDDC's planning committee had been opened to the public in 1986. Formal and informal consultation with residents increased. Slowly relationships improved yet more. The officers of the LDDC and the local authorities were anxious to talk to each other. Eventually all three local authorities once again took up their seats on the board of LDDC.

'Activity on the ground' slowly changed the perception of the local authorities to the plans of the LDDC. By 1993, Chairman Sir Michael Pickard could pleasingly observe in his report that 'Relations between the LDDC and local councils are cordial, co-operation between us smooth and agreement on our joint objectives mutual.'

The LDDC operated under some major constraints. For one, it was not a transport authority, a responsibility that remained with the local authorities (and the GLC up until 1986); yet it was crucial that the roads and the public transport network were brought up to the standard of other parts of London. It could not directly undertake improvements in housing and other community amenities; yet major improvements in these areas were essential. Education, too, remained the domain of the local authorities.

Right: As this advertisement of 1987 discloses, the area was not slow in promoting its future.

Left: **Peoples' politics: the citizens of Docklands were keen to make their views felt.**

So the LDDC had to proceed by acting as a catalyst and initiator. It necessarily had to be a partner – working with the government, with local agencies and the private sector. And to do so it also had to promote Docklands as desirable. Instead of continuing to view Docklands as a dinosaur, a defunct legacy of a bygone age, businesses, property developers, commuters, professional men and women, local people, those who had previously abandoned the area and local politicians needed to see it as an opportunity for success. Job creation needed confidence, and the LDDC needed to create that confidence.

No one can deny that the slum clearance policies of the post-Second World War years, with all its merits, had irrevocably destroyed some priceless legacies of Docklands' heritage. Only in the late 1970s did a new awareness of what was being lost slowly emerge. Even then, a priority was still to fill in the increasingly redundant docks, a policy halted only with the advent of the LDDC. Pride in these waters, rather than a plan to obliterate them wholesale, was new, though naturally many of the remaining residents remembered them with nostalgia.

For the most part, residents of Docklands were more than pleased with the visible results increasingly displayed as a result of the activities of the LDDC. The massive increase in employment, from 27,000 jobs in 1981 to nearly 72,000 in 1997; 15,700 new homes built, sold and occupied and nearly 6,000 social housing units built in the same era; the creation of 22 kilometres (13½ miles) of riverside walkway, which previously had almost all been inaccessible to the general public; new restaurants, shops, hotels, refurbished pubs and city farms; a revitalized transport system in an area which, for example, before the opening of the Docklands Light Railway had been serviced by an inadequate bus service; all this inevitably changed the perception of the general public to the work of the LDDC. The general public had and has voting influence over local authorities. The local authorities remembered that the LDDC had, as well as funds, a limited lifetime. Eventually its powers would be handed back, and its achievements handed over: such achievements as the 1990 £14.5 million extension to Tower Hamlets post-16 college, of which £10 million came from the exchequer of the LDDC.

In consequence of this decision to 'co-habit', joint schemes set up between the LDDC and the local authorities emerged. A social compact with Newham – the Memorandum of Agreement – for example, gave this authority an entrée to what was going to regenerate Docklands. In return for Newham's support for large development schemes planned at the time in the Royal Docks, the LDDC pledged to work with the council to secure benefits for local residents in the new Docklands: 1,500 new homes for rent in the area were targeted; jobs would be secured for local people in the new schemes, and training given to equip people with the right skills. There would also be a range of community and leisure facilities funded, including new schools, health centres and sports facilities. Sir Christopher Benson, the then Chairman of the LDDC, congratulated the negotiating teams on both sides and gave his opinion that 'this is the beginning of a long and fruitful partnership'.

In any event, those schemes were never built, victims of the late 1980s' recession, but the LDDC and the borough stuck to their agreement, working towards the goal of securing the targets laid down in the compact. By 1997 these had virtually all been achieved.

In Tower Hamlets a Liberal Democrat administration took over in 1987, and proved more accommodating than the previous administration. An Accord was signed. The council agreed to support the LDDC's major road construction programme, including a 1.8 km (1 mile)-long tunnel to be built under Limehouse Basin. In its path were a number of council blocks – some 169 flats.

Under the Accord the LDDC agreed to rehouse those tenants and people from a further 296 units as well as a number of families who were sharing homes. In all 556 households were rehoused, the majority in new housing association properties, while some opted for refurbished council homes.

The LDDC paid for the new housing association properties, the majority at Timber Wharves on the Isle of Dogs. It also compensated the council with £96,000 for each vacated council flat, and paid for secondary glazing in other properties and for the temporary rehousing of some families while the roads were built.

The rehousing of some of these families into 30 new homes at Lukin Street, Wapping, all with gardens and ranging in size from three to six bedrooms, was celebrated at the end of 1990 by a plaque unveiling ceremony by the Mayor of Tower Hamlets and the Chairman of the LDDC. Mayor Janet Ludlow declared that the East End had seen nothing like this rehousing since the Second World War. 'The Accord enables local people to share in the benefits of the enormous changes now taking place in our borough,' said the Mayor.

Rightly she took credit on behalf of the council for what had been done. 'We achieved a major coup in ensuring that they were housed in new properties.' The LDDC Chairman David Hardy equally exulted. 'The success of the rehousing

Right: A vital new thoroughfare: the Limehouse Link under construction at Limehouse Basin. This four-lane, cut-and-cover tunnel connects the Isle of Dogs to the City of London.

initiative in a joint venture between the Corporation and Tower Hamlets on the Isle of Dogs. As a sign of the times the Corporation and the borough had set up the Considerate Contractors Scheme in 1989 to ensure construction and maintenance in the area were carried out safely and with consideration to the public.

programme bears testament to the close co-operation between the LDDC and the council in providing the best permanent accommodation for the families affected by the Limehouse Link road scheme.' It was, he judged, a housing achievement unprecedented in Britain.

Criticisms of the LDDC and Tower Hamlets council were, said Councillor Brian Williams, the Chair of Tower Hamlets policy sub-committee, in 1988, 'groundless and mischievous'.

Southwark Council had been difficult to woo. In 1985 the Chairman of the LDDC, Sir Christopher Benson, had written to the leader of the council, Councillor Tony Ritchie, with the complaint, 'It has been a disappointment to us that up until now, unlike in Newham and Tower Hamlets, we have not achieved as many ... schemes as we would like to see in Southwark.' Discussions on housing policy had broken down three years previously. But in spite of Sir Christopher Benson's acerbity, they were starting up again.

By October 1994 Councillor Nick Dolezal, Chairman of the environmental committee of the borough of Southwark, was at Rotherhithe civic centre, handing out prizes to what were called 'Considerate Contractors'. The scheme had been funded jointly by Southwark Council and the LDDC, and followed the success of the

Left: **Governmental approval: the then Prime Minister, Margaret Thatcher, starts the work on the construction of the Limehouse Link, 1989.**

Yet it was not enough for the LDDC to woo the Docklands borough councils; the local community also had to be won over. The rapid pace of change in Docklands and extensive commercial development left some residents feeling excluded. Dissent often manifested into action: the visit of Robin Leigh-Pemberton, the Governor of the Bank of England, to Canary Wharf in the mid-1980s took on a surreal air when it was disrupted by the release of sheep and bees from the local urban farm.

In 1996 the Corporation commissioned MORI to conduct a survey to gauge the attitudes of local residents to its achievements. It was now ten years since Bow MP Ian Mikardo had memorably described the LDDC as 'a bejewelled harlot who provides instant attraction, but no long-term satisfaction'. How had the public's perception of the LDDC changed in the interim? MORI discovered that in the two years previous to 1996 more people had come to think that their quality of life had improved. The happiest

Below: The way we were: the back of Mellish Street, Isle of Dogs, looking north towards a Docklands undergoing regeneration, c.1989.

Below: **Popular
protest: Bowley
Street, a derelict site
off Westferry Road,
in the late 1980s.**

Below: Late-nineteenth-century terraced houses in Manchester Road, Isle of Dogs, whose inhabitants also failed to welcome the work of the LDDC.

lived in Surrey Docks, the least happy in the Royal Docks and on the Isle of Dogs. But those who believed that the LDDC had done a good job outnumbered those who disagreed by five to one.

These statistics need to be carefully interpreted. Surrey Docks has a high proportion of renters, many of them young people on high incomes. And the views of the minority are also important. Two out of ten people living in London's Docklands believe that since the early 1980s their standard of life has declined. To justify this view, they point to dirt and air pollution, to crime, to unemployment (especially in the Royal Docks), to traffic problems and to – significantly for the contribution of the LDDC – over-development.

Yet two out of three docklanders believed in 1996 that the LDDC had done its job well, and only one in four persons interviewed said they had scarcely any confidence in the Corporation. Three out of the five interviewees held that the local community had benefited from the work of the LDDC, and 16 per cent proclaimed their belief that the local community had benefited greatly.
As for housing, many believed that since the inauguration of the LDDC this key feature of the Docklands had much improved.

East-Enders remained themselves – far from subservient. In March 1997 the LDDC nearly lost a battle with some of them and their MPs over a plot of land at Hermitage Wharf in Wapping. The LDDC planned to sell this land, close to Tower Bridge, to be redeveloped as riverside flats, as shops and as restaurants. Residents vigorously opposed the plan. The area was festooned with ribbons, flowers and posters, all demanding instead of these a park, to commemorate civilians who died during the Second World War.

The results of a public inquiry into the plans appeared to support the demands not for housing but for a memorial park.

Docklands' citizens, it seemed, had demonstrated that Docklands belonged to them, not to the LDDC. Alas, the residents had not read the small print of the judgement, and the LDDC sold the land.

Yet a compromise emerged. The developers redrew their plans to include up to half for a memorial park. Local wishes and the need to regenerate a large tract of development land had both been taken into account, although the residents continued to campaign for the park and against the development.

4

...We see no more

Green lanes, but alleys dark instead,

Where none can walk but fear to tread

On babes that crawl in dirt and slime.

And from thy windows, at this time,

Thou canst not see ten yards beyond,

For the high blocks that stand around;

Buildings that ofttimes only give

One room in which five souls must live.

Foul art thou now with lives of care,

For hungry children and men poor

Seek food and lodging at thy door;

Thou that didst hear, in thy first hours,

Birds sing, and saw the sweet wild flowers.

W. H. Davies

The Local Community

Opposite: **Nature and human handiwork at one: a swan swims placidly at Lavender Pond, within view of Canary Wharf's tower.**

Poet and mariner W. H. Davies's words are a reminder that life was not always idyllic for the people of London's docklands. Their employers could be rapacious. For example, until a long-overdue Protective Act was passed in 1843, seamen, waterside workers and the Thames coal-whippers were in many ways at the mercy of local publicans. They found employment unloading barrels of beer and other victuals only if these publicans gave it to them; and the publicans would employ only those who agreed to spend 50 per cent of their wages in the public houses.

And there were other hazards to a dock worker's earnings. In his *London Labour and the London Poor*, published in the mid-nineteenth century, Henry Mayhew noted that an easterly wind, closing the Thames to traffic, would instantly put 20,000 dockers out of work.

These docks had already attracted many virtually destitute workers and their families. In the late eighteenth century workers from the North, made redundant by technical developments in the cotton and woollen industries such as the

spinning jenny and the flying shuttle, migrated south to find employment. In the nineteenth century, Irish men and women, driven from their land by poverty and the potato famine, crossed the sea and found their way to the docks. For many the conditions in which they now led their lives were wretched, their housing frightful. Hippolyte Taine's *Notes*

sur Angleterre, which appeared in 1871, described their 'narrow lodgings, sometimes merely single rooms where everyone huddles in the foul air'. These, he observed, were mostly one-storeyed, low and narrow – mere dens. He discovered families whose bed was a mere heap of soot. Next Charles Booth, himself a shipping magnate, described in his *Life and Labour of the London Poor* (which he began to publish in 1889) the miseries of some 75,000 people, most of them dockers, coal-heavers and waterside porters whose work was seasonal, casual and absurdly intermittent. He described a dock labourer whose wife was consumptive. Other dockers' families, he found, were not so destitute, one labourer earning 21 shillings a week, which was supplemented by what his wife earned by needlework.

But times became yet more difficult. The dock companies were stressed by mutual rivalry. Striking dockers added to their problems. The dockers' leader was John Burns, a former engineer. Socialists had convened meetings at the dock gates for several years before the great strike of August 1889. Few dockers joined their ranks, until the gasworkers successfully formed a union. Now lightermen and stevedores stopped work in protest against their miserable wages and the system of casual labour. Throughout the strike Burns kept order among the dockers by appearing among them wearing a straw hat. Daily he organized processions through the City of London. His ally, Tom Mann, like Burns a former engineer, issued food tickets to those in need.

Above: **Traditional sports still prosper in Docklands, as this picture of Millwall Park Bowling Green shows.**

Below: The new Docklands rises from the past: Canary Wharf's tower dominates the skyline, but at the local allotments, life goes on.

Even some of the dock directors were moved, contributing to a total of £13,700 given to the dockers by the general public. British trades unions and trades councils donated another £4,600. Australian allies of the striking dockers contributed a staggering £30,000. The strike was ultimately successful when the Roman Catholic Cardinal Archbishop of Westminster, Henry Edward Manning, came out on the side of the dockers, many of whom were Irish immigrants belonging to the Catholic flocks of London. John Burns announced that the strike had won for the dockers a wage of sixpence an hour, or as he put it, 'the full round orb of the dockers' tanner'. A dockers' union was now established, with Tom Mann as its President. By 1901 this Dock, Wharf, Riverside and General Workers' Union boasted nearly 14,000 members.

All was not yet won – witness the fact that another dockers' leader, Ben Tillett, a former sailor who would later become a Labour MP, was expelled from Hamburg and Antwerp in 1896 for supporting dockers' strikes there. But the dockers' leaders were increasingly flexing their muscles. In 1892 John Burns had been elected Labour MP for Battersea and would eventually become President of the Local Government Board and subsequently President of the Board of Trade (resigning when the First World War broke out). No member of the British working classes had ever become a Cabinet Minister before

Left: **An historic photograph: stevedores gather with their ship 'float' during the 1889 Dock Strike, when they demanded, amongst other things, a minimum engagement of four hours a day.**

Burns. He believed that all the dock companies needed to be merged into one municipal body. He astutely perceived (as a Royal Commission of 1902 agreed) that the docks were now ill-run and inefficient and were losing trade to foreign companies. The Royal Commission recommended that a new port authority should be constituted.

Eventually, in part because of his pressure, the Port of London Authority took control of the river and its docks in 1909. Under its sway, docking charges were reduced and parts of the Thames were dredged, as were some of the docks. By 1939 9.6 kilometres (6 miles) of quayside had been built and 32 hectares (80 acres) of new dock water dredged.

But life was still not idyllic for dockers. Stevedores were 'called' (in the phrase of the time) at various points. In the Royal Docks this spot was in a fenced enclosure by a railway crossing on the Connaught Road. For those who wanted work in the Surrey Docks, the assembly point was in Redriff Road. Dockers wanting work in the West India and Millwall Docks had to gather at three calling-on places. Beside all these calling-on places were coffee shops and pubs, the latter licensed to open as early as six o'clock in the morning, particularly to cater for those who didn't find work.

But a hundred or so years later the circumstances in which East-Enders lived needed serious upgrading, particularly with regard to housing. The LDDC set about promoting this. The LDDC was never a housing authority, for the statutory provision remained with the local authorities. However, the Corporation had to ensure that, within its regeneration

In the mid-nineteenth century Henry Mayhew described these extraordinary scenes. Masses of men, 'of all grades, looks and kinds, some in dirty shirts, others with waistcoats fastened up to the throat, would congregate at the gates of the docks'. As the calling foremen made their appearance these men, hoping for work, would rush to their locations. Then, Mayhew observed, began 'the scuffling and scrambling forth of them'. 'Many of them, it was clear,' he recorded, 'came to the gate without the means of a day's meal, and being hired, were obliged to go on credit for the very food they worked upon.'

Some dockers had benefited from the work of a few enlightened philanthropists, such as Samuel Augustus Barnett, vicar of St Jude's, Whitechapel, from 1872 to 1894, who helped to promote the Artisans' Dwelling Act of 1875. Two years later he and his wife Henrietta founded the Children's Holiday Movement. He helped to set up Toynbee Hall, the Universities' Settlement in East London, and was its first warden. His parish library was the basis of Whitechapel Public Library, and his art exhibitions eventually resulted in the building of Whitechapel Art Gallery.

Left: **Many 'hands' were needed to preserve the proud boast that Docklands made London the emporium of the world. This photograph of a meat-porter on a ship in the Royal Docks was taken in the mid-1930s.**

remit, housing was available to encourage people to live and work in the area. Its role, therefore, was as a catalyst: marketing its own sites for private house building and social housing schemes, planning developments, contributing grants to housing associations and to the boroughs to refurbish existing local authority homes, and thus providing local residents with the opportunity to buy their own homes.

Below: After a visit to a Port of London Authority warehouse in 1914, the poet laureate, John Masefield, wrote that such buildings housed 'the wealth of the world and London's power'.

Following this policy, between its inception and 1988 the LDDC had stimulated the building of 7,000 new homes. Of these, 4,000 had been sold to locals, most of them at less than £40,000, in line with the Corporation's 'affordable housing policy', a policy established in the 1980s specifically to enable local people to buy their own homes.

When the LDDC was set up, 95 per cent of Docklands' 15,000 homes were rented, almost all from the three local authorities of Newham, Southwark and Tower Hamlets. The statistics are fascinating. In 1981, out of Docklands' mere 14,881 homes, only 784 of these were owner-occupied – 449 in Newham, 262 in Tower Hamlets and 73 in Southwark. A staggering 93 per cent of residents of Bermondsey Riverside lived in rented council property, with a trivial 2 per cent owning homes. And yet some influential leaders wanted to fill in some of the docks, to provide yet more council houses. By contrast, a crucial aim of the LDDC was to achieve a different, more balanced mix, with local people and newcomers to Docklands given the chance of renting, buying their homes, or else taking up the option of shared ownership (whereby the occupier buys a share in the property and rents the remainder). The policy worked. By the end of 1997 some 43 per cent of the homes in the locality were owner-occupied.

By this time more than 21,600 new homes had been built. Of these, 15,600 were now privately owned; 5,000 had been built by housing associations and almost 1,000 by the local authorities. Construction of social housing had been stimulated by LDDC finance, which had pumped in more than £180 million to build new homes or replace old ones. Almost half of the new housing association homes (2,000) had been secured with the help of LDDC grants of more than £50 million.

The emphasis on mixed development was the key to the 1985 'Downtown Package', an agreement reached between the LDDC, Southwark Council and a number of housing associations and developers. Under the terms of the agreement, the Corporation paid the council £3 million for seven run-down and derelict estates, enabling the council to spend the cash on

much-needed refurbishment of other estates in the area. The derelict blocks were then transformed into high-quality, modern housing for rent, shared ownership and open-market sales.

The image of London Docklands at the beginning of the 1980s was not one that tempted builders to venture their capital. Under the impetus of Reg Ward, the LDDC's first Chief Executive, builders Barratt, Wimpey, Broseley and Comben were persuaded to create new homes for sale on a 12-hectare (30-acre) site at Beckton. Somewhat surprisingly, all the homes were pre-sold, and the builders asked for more land. As the remit of the LDDC came to its end, the ratio of owner-occupiers to council house tenants in Beckton was higher than anywhere else in the Urban Development Area.

Opposite:
New housing in Docklands: a crescent in Beckton.
Above: **Some docklanders took care of their own future by building their own homes.**

'If Beckton is associated with one single achievement in the life of the Corporation, it has to be new homes for sale,' judged Eric Sorensen in 1997. He added that the development was the culmination of over 14 years of co-operation with the London Borough of Newham and with the fast-growing local community.

And its success not only encouraged the Corporation to release other land for housing throughout the Urban Development Area but also attracted more developers to build homes in Docklands. Six new sites, envisaging 936 homes, were inaugurated in the following two years, mostly in Newham, the rest in Southwark. A further 954 were envisaged: more for Beckton, others for Wapping, Southwark and the Isle of Dogs.

Thus the Corporation, acting as a vital catalyst, also worked hand in hand with such house builders as Barrat, Wimpey, Persimmon Homes (in the beginning known as Ideal Homes) and Regalian to stimulate new housing throughout Docklands. Eventually such initiatives resulted in accommodation ranging from houses costing as little as £28,000 to apartments costing from £300,000, whose privileged residents could view Tower Bridge. The conversion of warehouses into housing continued apace. The success of the LDDC in stimulating jobs and thus attracting people back into London Docklands – with a staggering population growth from 39,400 in 1981 to some 80,000 in 1997 – made the housing task yet more vital. Building continued.

The speed at which regeneration took place also played its role in the look of parts of the new Docklands. The first luxury housing development on the Isle of Dogs was Cascades. The building does

indeed seem to cascade at one end. The brief for Cascades was given at the end of January 1986. Planning permission was given in October. The building was completed within 18 months. Some like its naval overtones – the portholes, ships' bridges and turrets built into the scheme. It has also been described as 'architectural misbehaviour'.

Left: Terraced cottages built in the 1920s and 1930s offer a haven of tranquility in Docklands. A sea of 'For Sale' signs denotes the 1980s' housing boom. *Right:* Cascades, a residential building in Westferry Road. The nautical elements – portholes, turrets and ships' bridges – fittingly mirror its waterside site.

Other housing developments were humane and delightful. A Dutch company, VOM of Amsterdam, built a charming complex on the Isle of Dogs which includes Van Gogh Court, Amsterdam Road and Rotterdam Road.

So local communities were enhanced. In 1994 West Silvertown was isolated, with a mere 260 council flats, 60 privately-owned homes and few job opportunities. In March 1994 the first phase of West Silvertown Urban Village was launched, consisting of 85 Peabody Trust homes for renting to local people. Tate & Lyle, the Peabody Trust, the London Borough of Newham and the LDDC also planned an urban village to be built here over eight to ten years on a 31.5-hectare (78-acre) site, which would house up to 5,000 people and provide them with shops, recreational facilities and workplaces.

Left: **The Barley Mow Estate in Limehouse, refurbished with the help of the LDDC.**

Dickon Robinson, the Director of Development for Peabody Trust, declared: 'This new urban village is making a break with town planning trends since the 1960s, which have tended to segment areas into business parks, residential and leisure areas. It will be a balanced community, where people will be able to live, work and enjoy recreational facilities in close proximity.' He went on to comment: 'Urban villages could not be more timely as concern mounts over environmental problems, such as traffic pollution; they reduce the need for the motor car as people will have access to homes, jobs, shops and leisure facilities all within easy walking distance.' By 1996 the Environment Secretary and Minister for London, John Gummer, was unveiling a commemorative flagstone on the quayside of Royal Victoria Dock to mark the start of construction of 235 new homes for rent at Britannia Village, the first major part of West Silvertown Urban Village. These new homes would join 777 private houses and quayside apartments already under construction.

Stimulating the provision of new homes went hand in hand with the necessary improvement of older ones. In Limehouse, for example, on the Barley Mow estate 180 council homes, built in the 1960s, were refurbished at a cost of £10½ million in 1993, following construction of the Limehouse Link Tunnel through the area. The money was provided by the government's estate action programme, by Tower Hamlets council and by the LDDC.

One problem arose between 1989 and 1993 from the LDDC's constuction of the Limehouse Link, which required the demolition of 169 homes, largely on the Barley Mow Estates in Limehouse. Whatever the benefits of the Link in terms of business and easing traffic problems, some of those whose lives were disrupted were understandably angry. LDDC and Tower Hamlets council joined hands to try to alleviate their plight, and signed a ground-breaking agreement known as The Accord. In return for the council's co-operation over the LDDC's road-building schemes, the Corporation agreed to fund a £35 million package of social, economic and community projects in the borough, and to provide new accommodation and refurbished homes for council tenants directly affected by the Link. The LDDC also agreed to rehouse people from an additional 296 units and a number of families who were sharing homes. In total 556 households were moved; secondary glazing was provided in 338 homes; and 301 council homes were refurbished. Most of the rehoused families were offered new housing association homes, mainly on the Isle of Dogs, while some opted for refurbished council homes. The cost for the LDDC was over £100 million.

As for the health of the citizens of Docklands, by March 1997 the Corporation had helped in the building of five health centres and the refurbishing of six others. The costs were considerable – £525,000 to a major new health facility, Island Health, on the Isle of Dogs; £125,000 to the new

Docklands Medical Centre, in the south-west of the Isle of Dogs; £430,000 towards the new health centre at Newby Place, Poplar; £175,000 towards the redevelopment of Kennard Street Health Centre in North Woolwich; £150,000 towards the extension of Albion Health Centre in Rotherhithe. Another contribution, this one of £700,000, was made to the Royals medical centre in East Beckton, which was planned to accommodate four GPs, a dentist, community health staff and a pharmacist. In Mill Street, Bermondsey (a street which derives its name from a water-mill set up by medieval monks), the LDDC helped to fund a new doctors' surgery as well as helping to refurbish the John Dixon Clinic.

People need not only decent homes and health facilities but also a humane environment. Parks, landscaping and play areas all contribute to this, and the LDDC paid out over £42 million towards creating such amenities. In 1997 in the Royal Docks an 8.8-hectare (22-acre) park was being laid out beside the Thames Barrier, designed by the Paris firm Groupe Signes and the London-based urban designers Patel Taylor. The plan envisages a riverside promenade and new housing. The LDDC have contributed to the project: following the Corporation's demise, money will be available through English Partnerships

(a body set up by the government in 1993 to regenerate derelict, under-used and vacant land, and which will take over the LDDC's contractual responsibilities and land holdings in the Royal Docks). Eventually this park will be handed over to the London Borough of Newham.

One of Docklands' early success stories is the regeneration of Beckton. The Royal Docks aside, this region was once noted chiefly as the destination of London's

sewage (boasting Europe's largest sewage treatment works) and for possessing Europe's largest gasworks (hence the name of the district, after Simon Adams Beck, first Governor of the gasworks). Beckton's last major development before the creation of the LDDC had been the Cyprus housing estate, built in 1881, after the Royal Albert Dock opened, and named after the island which the British had taken over three years earlier.

By 1981 the London Borough of Newham had, however, set its mind to improving Beckton's environment and services. The marshes had been drained and a new drainage system installed. New council houses were under construction, and the building of a couple of new schools was well in hand. But the gasworks had closed down. Late in 1981 the Port of London Authority closed down the Royal Docks. The population was declining, to a low of 5,106 in 1981. The residents were served by a few parades and by corner shops.

Left above: **Island Health, Isle of Dogs, provides a work base for up to 70 permanent and visiting health professionals.**

Left below: **St John's Park, Isle of Dogs – a safe place for children to play.**

The LDDC was able to build on and also modify these initiatives, above all, as we have seen, by aiming to encourage private occupiers of new houses. Likewise local housing associations were encouraged. And by 1997 three primary schools had been built for Beckton alone, as well as a church centre, children's play areas, three community centres and two health centres – all stimulated by LDDC initiatives and cash. The Royal Docks Medical Centre in Cyprus alone benefited from a grant of £700,000; St Mark's community centre from £1.4 million; Winsor Park community centre from £446,000.

The remit was bringing in results. Docklands Light Railway reached Beckton in March 1994. In 1997 a new river crossing was planned at Gallions Reach, to connect the A13 in the north with the A2016 in Thamesmead. If built, it is estimated that the crossing will encourage development creating up to 16,000 new jobs.

The local community in other areas of Docklands also benefited from the LDDC's policies. The Corporation realized that training and education were clearly priorities in areas (such as Bermondsey Riverside) where up to 60 per cent of the population were long-term unemployed. A construction training centre, an IT computer training centre and other such projects received £846,000 from the funds of the LDDC. In addition, £439,000 was donated towards the Bermondsey site of Southwark College, and £263,000 to the Butlers Wharf Chef School, which opened in 1996 and guarantees a quota of places to local people.

Fittingly, in view of its Chef School, Bermondsey (once described by Charles Dickens as 'the filthiest, the strangest, the most extraordinary of the many localities

that are hidden in London') is today a district of fine restaurants and food shops. Warehouses have been renamed (by Sir Terence Conran) Cardamon, Clove, Cinnamon, Nutmeg and Coriander. Here too is the Bramah Tea and Coffee Museum. Shad Thames (whose name derives from the twelfth-century Knights Templar of St John at Thames) has risen again.

As for schools in Bermondsey, between 1981 and 1996 St Joseph's RC Primary School received £75,000, Riverside Primary School £35,000 and St Michael's RC Secondary School £34,000. Bermondsey nursery schools were helped, as were the district's youth and community centres and the Scout House building in Jamaica Road.

Above: Self-building was one method of regenerating London Docklands; this photograph shows some of the pioneers.
Right: Maconochie's Wharf, an example of the results of 'self-building' schemes in Docklands.

Borough of Tower Hamlets and the Church Urban Fund, we have a chance to cater for all needs within our local community.' Skillnet, a Docklands-based training organization, and Grand Metropolitan Training were also planning to operate from the centre and pledged to contribute £40,000 a year to its upkeep.

The 1989 Accord agreed between the LDDC and Tower Hamlets to facilitate the Corporation's road-building schemes proved profitable for the council. In 1991 the then Minister of State for the Environment, Michael Portillo, planted a time capsule when the LDDC formally handed over the new £14.5 million Tower Hamlets College Extension to the local education authority. The LDDC had contributed £10 million towards the cost of this extension, some £8 million of this derived from the £35 million promised under the terms of the Social Accord. In May 1991 an old school building in Wapping, owned by St Peter's Church, was opened as a completely refurbished community centre. The church had raised £100,000 towards the scheme. The LDDC contributed approximately £1 million. Local residents' associations, dance classes, medical and childcare facilities, drama clubs and staff facilities for nearby businesses were now available. As the parish priest, Father Derek Peel, put it, 'Together with the LDDC, the London

Left: A commitment to education in Docklands: Tower Hamlets College was just one of the recipients of LDDC grants.

Above right: By 1991 the Docklands Computer-Aided Learning Programme had helped to provide 550 computers for schools in Tower Hamlets and Southwark.

Another 1991 initiative for young people was the creation, with LDDC money, of the Millwall Estate Playground in Westferry Road. Toddlers and children up to the age of 11 were here provided with vandal-proof climbing frames. Here too were bouncy toys, slides, tyre swings and a safety-play surface – the whole designed in consultation with the local tenants' association.

With the coming of new businesses, new jobs were being created and training became a priority. Of the over-16 pupils in Docklands, 70 per cent were now taking advantage of 2,000 further education places. 'Training is central to the objectives of the Corporation in securing lasting social and economic regeneration within Docklands,' commented Bob Pringle,

then LDDC's Director of Community Infrastructure. 'We recognize that it is essential that local people of all ages and backgrounds are equipped with the skills required to share in the benefits of the development of this area.'

It was a major challenge for the Corporation to help Docklands' residents secure employment and to ensure that the area's employers were able to recruit locally. This it did by acting as a catalyst, by working with the statutory providers, the local education authorities and the Training and Enterprise Councils. In the short term, a range of programmes was put in place to train people for the new jobs in Docklands. These varied from programmes in basic skills to customized training – tailoring courses to meet the needs of individual employers – and a broad range of vocational training, from childcare training to construction, hotel and catering and information technology training. But there was also a long-term investment to be made in education in the area.

Traditionally the area's main sources of employment, the docks, had not demanded high educational achievement. The new employers – operating in banking, finance, insurance, business services and publishing – had greater expectations. By 1997 the academic performance of the area's schools had started to improve significantly, with a huge increase in the number of pupils staying on past 16 to gain better qualifications.

By 1997 the LDDC had helped fund 11 new primary schools and two new secondary schools, extensions and refurbishments of a further 12, as well as contributing to three post-16 colleges – one in each of the three Docklands boroughs – and nine vocational training centres.

The LDDC set about promoting computer literacy in the urban development area's primary and secondary schools. By 1991 the Docklands Computer-Aided Learning Project, set up three years previously, had provided a total of 550 computers for 33 primary, secondary and special schools in Tower Hamlets and Southwark, thus benefiting around 7,800 pupils. The cost was some £2 million, with another £400,000 provided by the Inner London Education Authority and the London Boroughs of Tower Hamlets and Southwark.

It seemed also right to extend this programme to parents as well as children, so after-school activities now included word-processing, second language learning, and the learning of such mother tongues as Bengali. In consequence some schools stayed open after hours, to provide equipment and expertise for the local community.

Having proved so successful in Tower Hamlets and Southwark, the computer project was next extended to schools in the London Borough of Newham. In all, £4 million was spent on computers in 52 schools, giving Docklands the best computer-to-pupil ratio in the UK.

This was but one of the LDDC's commitments to education. By the time the Computer-Aided Learning programme was set up, in September 1995 to boost reading standards amongst seven-year-olds, the Corporation has already spent some £30 million in educating local people.

Above: **Students outside Bacon's City Technology College, Surrey Docks.**
Right: **New schools, such as Bluegate Fields, Wapping, were vital to improve the education of Docklands' children.**

Below: Yet more facilities for young people: Island Baths, Isle of Dogs.

Opposite above: An intrepid climber at Limehouse Youth Club. *Opposite below:* In the past, timber was temporarily stored on Lavender Pond, Rotherhithe. Today the pond is an ecological delight.

Support for schools, to meet the needs of the growing Docklands' population, was one of the earliest LDDC initiatives. £450,000 was made available for Beckton's Ellen Wilkinson Primary School, which opened in 1987. In 1994, with LDDC support, building began on two new primary schools: the first was Alfred Salter School in Surrey Docks; the second, at Arnhem Wharf, was the first such school to be built on the Isle of Dogs for over 20 years. In 1996 three Wapping primary schools were improved and Bacon's City Technology College in the Surrey Docks extended.

The Corporation gave a substantial grant to building a swimming pool for St Luke's Primary School in Saunders Ness Road. It helped with the costs of the new Winsor Primary School in Beckton, with some imagination, its grant including provision for a parents' room and family centre, as well as landscaped playing fields and a nature pool. As for secondary and higher education, the LDDC has helped to fund Newham Sixth Form College and Newham College of Further Education, Bacon's City Technology College, Tower Hamlets College, as well as the University of East London's new Docklands campus in the Royal Docks.

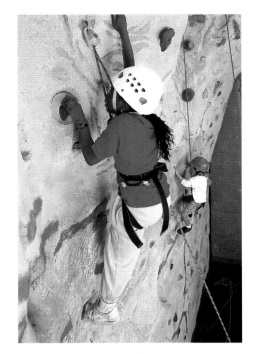

The provision of leisure facilities was another important factor in the regeneration of Docklands. In Bermondsey, for example, the London Dungeon, the Design Museum, Hay's Galleria and HMS *Belfast* were promoted as delights designed to attract visitors to the area. Tower Bridge Piazza (once the Courage brewery), Anchor Brewhouse, Butlers Wharf and New Concordia Wharf were both transformed and yet conserved. Offices were developed, mainly between Tower Bridge and London Bridge, and 333 local authority homes were refurbished in Bermondsey Riverside, partly funded by an LDDC investment of £3.9 million.

As the end of its remit approached, the LDDC continued to fund watersports. In June 1997, after an injection of £800,000 from the Corporation, Docklands Watersports Club's new floating clubhouse, the *Tereza Joanne*, was launched at the King George V Dock. This converted and refurbished sheer-leg lifting barge, weighing 400 tonnes, has wet and dry changing-rooms, a promenade deck and accommodation for the owners and staff. Primarily aimed at its private members, focusing on jet skiing and wet biking, it nevertheless opens its bar and restaurant to the general public, who can also hire jet skis, after the necessary training, which is also provided by the club.

The Corporation envisaged leisure marching hand in hand with ecology. In consequence, the LDDC has planted more than 160,000 trees. Its first ecological project was the William Curtis Ecology Park, which transferred to Stave Hill in Surrey Docks in 1981, on to 2.2 hectares (5½ acres) of land leased from the LDDC. These docks now also incorporate Lavender Pond and Russia Dock Woodland. Elsewhere the banks of ponds and canals were replanted. Rare plants began to grow. Soon over 24 of the 57 native species of British butterfly were spotted at Stave Hill and in the Russia Dock Woodland.

As part of a 1994 landscaping project, the Corporation provided a 12-metre (39-foot)-high wind-power turbine for Stave Hill. It pumps a continuous supply of high-quality water from a depth of 60 metres (197 feet) to feed the linked ponds. Previously the water came from the mains system and was both expensive and ecologically impure. 'The building of the wind turbine and complementary landscaping represents just part of the Corporation's on-going commitment to protecting and enhancing the natural environment, so it can be enjoyed by people living and working in the area today and in the future,' said Jeff Hennessey, the LDDC's City Design Manager.

Involving the local community in such projects was increasingly seen as a priority, and when Bow Creek ecology park – London's sole urban wetland – opened in 1994, local children were invited to plant reeds in its pond. In due course young people would be invited to work its sluices and water-wheels. Since many citizens of Docklands live near water, watersports centres were also opened, eventually as many as 10 of them.

Mudchute Farm, Europe's largest urban farm, is one example of derelict or waste land put to innovative new use. Its history is bizarre: in the nineteenth century thousands of tonnes of silted mud were dredged out of Millwall Dock and

deposited on the eastern edge of East Ferry Road. The councillors of the borough of Poplar were ill-pleased and went so far as to sue the dock company for creating a health hazard for the local residents. As a result, dumping ceased. Slowly the silt hardened. Locals spotted that it was extremely fertile, and during the First World War they took it over as allotments.

Today Mudchute embraces stables, where each day horses are groomed and trotted. Birds abound; sheep and even a lama or two placidly graze on what was once the dumping ground of the excavated docks. In June 1991, a month before the tenth anniversary of the founding of the LDDC, a new multi-purpose stable-block was topped out. It had cost £617,400, with the LDDC contributing 75 per cent.

Above: One of Docklands' more bizarre sights: a lama from Mudchute Farm and Canary Wharf's tower silhouetted against the evening sky. *Right:* Stave Hill, a 2.2-hectare (5½-acre) ecological park at the heart of the peninsula of Surrey Docks, offers fabulous views of both Docklands and the City of London.

shrubs and hedging of holly, helped to transform the area. The railings and entrance gates are embellished with a rope motif (the field was once the site of a ropemakers' works). Its bandstand is supported on columns reclaimed from a nineteenth-century warehouse in St Katharine Docks. This park enlivens a delightful ensemble. The 'House they left

Newham City Farm is a similar achievement, its creation stimulated by grants from the LDDC. Yet another successful venture is the Docklands Equestrian Centre, which includes livery stables, an equestrian centre equipped to international competition standards and a riding school catering for disabled and disadvantaged children and adults. The Corporation has consistently supported this venture. In May 1997, for instance, Sir Michael Pickard presented the London Docklands Trophy to the winner of a competition here in which six Welsh cobs drove show wagons, each sponsored to the tune of £1,500 by six local companies (Charfleet Ltd, London City Airport, the Mirror Group, National Westminster Bank, SavaCentre and Thames Water), to raise funds for the school. HRH the Duke of Edinburgh presented each driver with a commemorative medallion and rosette.

1994 saw the opening of Ropemakers Field, built over the Limehouse Link tunnel on previously derelict ground. This new 1.5-hectare (3¾-acre) park, designed in consultation with local residents and planted with horse chestnuts, limes,

Behind' pub here was built in 1857, when it was called The Black Horse. Its present name derives from the fact that, sadly, the Victorian terrace in which it once stood has been demolished. And here the Hackney sculptor Jane Ackroyd created a bronze and stainless-steel statue of a herring gull to serve as the focal point of Narrow Street Square.

Today East India Dock Basin is being transformed into a wildfowl sanctuary. Along with Texaco and Littlejohn Fraser, the LDDC consulted with the Royal Society for the Protection of Birds in siting 12 nesting rafts in the docks. This once desolate spot is an inspired site for such rafts, for it lies on a route taken by birds as they migrate up the Thames and then follow the River Lea inland.

As a result common terns, not seen here for decades, have returned to Docklands. So have lapwings, cormorants, a rare pair of black redstarts, little ringed plovers, shags, shelducks, herring gulls, swifts and wagtails. In pursuit of this same policy, bird and bat nesting boxes have been erected throughout the region, one even sitting on the top of Canary Wharf tower.

Left: A gymkhana at Mudchute Farm, near Island Gardens on the Isle of Dogs. The name of this area derives from its former role as a repository of the fill and mud from excavated docks.

Above right: Bow Creek, part of the delta of the River Lea, and still navigable by small boats.

Entertainment, in part simply to serve local people, in part to help put London Docklands on the map, has also been a concern of the LDDC. Monthly concerts were sponsored at Cabot Hall, including such bands as the 1960s' chart-toppers the Searchers and the legendary US group the Drifters. 'Comedy Club at Cabot Hall' featured a series of stand-up comics. The

As well as a decent environment, in the late twentieth century people also need supermarkets. As Docklands was regenerated, the great chains saw their opportunity. First to come was Asda, which opened the first supermarket on the Isle of Dogs in 1983, then another in Beckton in 1986. Tesco opened at Surrey Quays in 1988, and a Tesco Metro at Canary Wharf in 1995. The Surrey Quays development by Slough Estates was particularly successful at attracting other retailers, such as British Home Stores. At Canary Wharf, Jaeger, Ryman, Boots, Austin Reed and Corney & Barrow's wine bar were among others to move in. Elsewhere Safeway moved into Wapping in 1992, and Kwiksave and Sainsbury's into Beckton in 1993.

Mixed development was one keynote. London Bridge City, a project of the St Martin's Property Group, was begun in the 1980s and its first phase finished in 1987, when 116,000 square metres (1,250,000 square feet) of development – offices, a hospital, apartments, leisure provision and shopping complexes – had been set up. St Martin's Square has colonnades and fountains. St Olaf's House, a splendid art deco survival, has also been restored with the aid of LDDC money. New St Martin's Square will in time offer easy access to London Bridge station.

Limehouse festival of 1994 took on a Chinese theme, with martial arts and lion dancers. Another venture in 1996 saw the LDDC and Greenwich joining forces to promote the Greenwich + Docklands International Festival. Parachuting teddy bears graced the LDDC's 1994 sport kite festival. A classic car rally was accompanied by a jazz band. Such ventures cost relatively little, but they added to the gaiety of Docklands life and helped put Docklands back on the map.

One imaginative venture was the creation of a dry ski slope known as Beckton Alps. Its basis is the waste tipped by the former Beckton gasworks. Under the stimulus of the LDDC the massive tip was compacted, and then, with the help of the private sector and government grants, turned into a ski slope.

Another innovative measure to enhance life in Docklands, both for visitors and for the local community, was the LDDC's decision to sponsor sculpture. Dr Salter, the Docklands philanthropist, who lived from 1873 to 1945, was an obvious subject. Diane Gorvin was commissioned to sculpt him, and her bronze statue called 'Dr Salter Daydreams' now stands on Cherry Garden pier, Bermondsey. Naturally, Cumberland Wharf, whence the Pilgrim Fathers departed for New England in 1620, has a statue of one of them, with a boy and bull terrier, created by Peter McLean. At Canada Water is a statue of deal (i.e. timber) porters by Philip Bews. It playfully depicts their acrobatic skills. James Walker, the early-nineteenth-century engineer of Commercial Dock, is sculpted by Michael Rizello. John Rennie appears at Western Docks, sculpted by John Ravera.

Opposite: Surrey Quays Shopping Centre, which opened in late 1988, is enlivened with images of a former maritime era: lifebelts, rigging and ropes, as well as a dolphin statue.

Below: Waste from Beckton Gas Works was landscaped to build the dry ski slope known as Beckton Alps – an eyesore transformed into a delightful local amenity.

1 2 7

Not all of these delightful statues were commissioned by the LDDC. In the 1970s Taylor Woodrow commissioned David Wynne to create an exquisite 'Girl and Dolphin' for the riverside at St Katharine Docks. Outside the Design Museum at Shad Thames is a most bizarre combined head of Isaac Newton and James Watt. It lies on its side and was commissioned from the brilliant Edward Paolozzi by the Conran Foundation. The architects of Anchor Court (Wickham & Associates) commissioned the bronze torso from Anthony Donaldson which now entertains visitors to Tower Bridge piazza. David Backhouse's charming 'Fountains with Dolphins' at Surrey Quays shopping centre was commissioned by Tesco.

Fittingly, the Greater London Council commissioned Frank Foster to create the statue of the Labour leader Clement Attlee, which stands in front of Limehouse Library in Commercial Road. Equally fittingly, in stainless steel, horses by Brian Yale, another commission of the LDDC, prance on the Bridleway, Beckton Corridor. And, as a final bravura gesture, Seven Islands Leisure Centre is adorned with a mural by Rita Harris depicting a giant wave.

Museums were also seen as a means of enhancing local life. One important attraction is the floating museum of ships in St Katharine Docks. As well as contributing exhibition and revenue funding to The Design Museum, the LDDC also helped to fund the Passmore Edwards Museum in the former North Woolwich station, Pier Road, Newham, dedicated to the history of the Great Eastern railway.

Left: **Frank Foster's statue of Clement Attlee stands in Commercial Road outside Limehouse Library.**
Right: **In the past, Docklands timber porters (known as 'deal' porters) needed remarkable agility to do their work. In this statue at Canada Water, Surrey Docks, the sculptor Philip Bews has brilliantly captured their skills.**

Lastly, waterside pubs (and not only waterside ones, but also those set amid little local communities) were perceived as a boon. Naturally, Charles Dickens had perceived this too. 'Come, cheer up, my lads. We've the best liquors here,' he wrote in *The Uncommercial Traveller.* 'And you'll find something new in our wonderful Beer!' Almost certainly The Grapes is the pub he described in *Our Mutual Friend,* though he called it The Six Jolly Porters. In it he saw 'a bar to soften the human breast. The available space in it was not much larger than a hackney-coach; but no one could wish the bar bigger.'

frequented it. At the low-water mark just below the pub, rebellious mariners were hanged. The spectacle was a popular attraction, and in the seventeenth century the notorious Judge George Jeffreys frequently came along to watch. When he fell from grace, with the flight of his protector King James II, Jeffreys disguised himself as a sailor and followed

Here, Dickens wrote, were 'corpulent little casks' and 'cordial-bottles radiant with fictitious grapes in bunches'. Red curtains matched the noses of the clients. The landlady sat closer to the fire than anyone else. Here were lemons in nets and biscuits in baskets, as well as cheeses in a snug corner. Watermen used to climb up a ladder directly from the Thames into The Grapes.

Visit these pubs, then, to find glimpses of past times. The Mayflower, for example, was first built in 1550 (then called The Shippe) and stands by the jetty where the ship of the same name moored, before taking the Pilgrim Fathers on to Portsmouth and then to America. The Town of Ramsgate was founded in the 1460s and adopted its present name only in the nineteenth century, when Ramsgate fishermen began landing their catches at Wapping wharf.

But the oldest riverside pub in London, at 57 Wapping Wall, is The Prospect of Whitby. Built around 1520, the inn soon became notorious for the riff-raff that

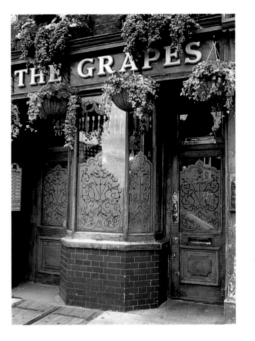

his royal master in attempting to flee the country. Ironically, he was captured at Wapping, and transferred to the Tower of London (a kindly act, since otherwise the mob would have lynched him), where he died in 1689.

More peacable visitors have relished The Prospect of Whitby, among them Samuel Pepys. Its present aspect is not that of the original, since the first pub was burned down and rebuilt. But it retains a venerable aspect, with its flagstoned floors, a pewter-topped counter supported on ancient barrels and rickety stairs

leading up to its restaurant, while the pub sign still depicts the sailing ship after which it is named. Inside, one chair bears the legend: 'This chair was occupied by HRH Princess Margaret when dining here on June 26, 1949.'

Not many years later, on 14 January 1953, Captain John Cunningham was giving a party in The Prospect of Whitby when the pub was raided by scoundrels led by Robert Harrington Saunders, who was known as 'Scarface'. Cunningham and his guests were forced to give up their money, jewellery and watches. Fortunately, Scarface was soon captured by the police. He shot one of them and was sentenced to life imprisonment. Old habits die hard in riverside pubs.

Left: **A delightful Docklands pub, The Grapes, in Narrow Street, Limehouse. The pub's timber veranda projects over the Thames.**
Right: **Probably the most famous Docklands' pub, the Prospect of Whitby. Haunt of such luminaries as Samuel Pepys, Judge Jeffreys and Rex Whistler, it began life in the 1520s as The Devil's Tavern.**

5

Earth has not anything to show more fair;

Dull would he be of soul who could pass by

A sight more touching in its majesty

This city now doth like a garment wear

The beauty of the morning; silent, bare,

Ships, towers, domes, theatres, and temples lie

Open unto the fields, and to the sky, –

All bright and glittering in the smokeless air...

William Wordsworth

Architecture, Design and Conservation

Opposite: Harbour Exchange, a vast office development completed in 1990, also incorporates restaurants, a pub and shops. Its promenade (where two dockside cranes have been preserved) offers an entrancing view of the former Millwall Inner Dock.

Wordsworth added: 'The river glideth at its own sweet will'. He was writing in 1802, and some of the towers included those of magical churches that still stand.

The supreme architectural treasures of London Docklands are three churches. Their architects were Nicholas Hawksmoor and John Walters. A Nottingham boy, Hawksmoor had the good fortune to work both for Sir Christopher Wren and Sir John Vanbrugh. He was also commissioned to build other notable London churches: St Mary Woolnoth, St George's, Bloomsbury, and Christ Church, Spitalfields.

These dockland buildings were called 'coal' churches, because some 50 of them were paid for by a tax levied on coal during the reign of Queen Anne. It was a profitable tax. As Daniel Defoe observed in his early-eighteenth-century *Tour Throughout the Whole Island of Great Britain*, at London could be seen 'the prodigious fleets of ships which come constantly with coals to this increasing city'.

Perhaps the finest of the classical coal churches designed for Docklands by Hawksmoor is St George in the East, in spite of the fact that Hitler's bombs destroyed its interior during the Second World War. Completed in 1729, this lovely building cost some £18,500, and boasts a tower rising to 55 metres (180 feet). Sir Joshua Reynolds designed its east windows. Its modern interior was the work of Arthur Bailey in the 1960s. The riveting nineteenth-century history of this church is beyond the scope of this book, but it is worth mentioning that its rector, espousing the causes both of the poor and of the new Catholic elements which were infiltrating into the Anglican Church and infuriating many, was immensely vilified and at one point even had his church closed down.

Close by St George in the East is Swedenborg Square. Now filled with local authority flats, it was once the site of the docklands' Swedish Church (which was demolished in 1937). Here was buried the Swedish philosopher and mystic Emmanuel Swedenborg, whose mortal remains were taken back to his homeland in 1908. And south of The Highway in Pennington

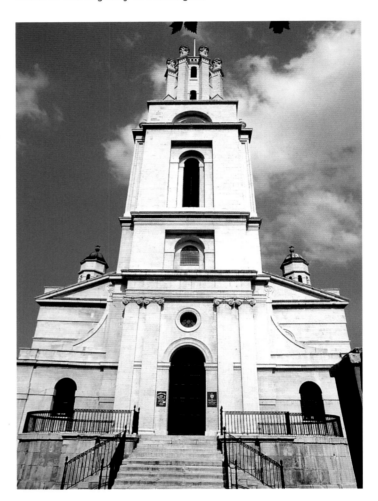

Left: Gleaming white, and yet a 'coal' church. Built in the reign of Queen Anne with money raised by a tax on coal, St George in the East, Wapping, was designed by Nicholas Hawksmoor and cost just over £18,500. *Right:* Another exquisite 'coal' church, St Anne's, Limehouse. Designed by Hawksmoor and completed in 1730, this church is beguiling, especially its interior, rebuilt in 1851 by the architect Philip Hardwick after the building was gutted by a fire.

Street are the offices of News International, which became known as 'Fortress Wapping' when *The Times* moved here in the early 1980s.

Maybe St George in the East is not Hawksmoor's loveliest East End church, for St Anne's, Limehouse, which was finished in 1730, is both exquisite and entrancingly complex. Like St George in

the East a coal church, it was built in open fields close by the Limehouse community of river workers. Today it sits at the end of a narrow cobbled street. Seven bays stretch themselves along the sides of the church, with God's acre enhanced by classical memorial stones. Its tower rises to two square, diagonally set stages, with four little square spires rising above them. At that time the church clock was the highest in London, and after Big Ben probably still is. The form of St Anne's is almost that of a Greek cross. After the Bishop had consecrated it, it is recorded that he drank some hot wine, took some sweetmeats, and when he had finished, the assembled clergy and laity scrambled for the rest.

Since St Anne's was built, two potential disasters have been surmounted. In the mid-nineteenth century the church caught fire. A sensitive London architect, Philip Hardwick (designer of Euston station, Goldsmith's Hall and the library and hall of Lincoln's Inn), restored it between 1851 and 1857, building a new font and pulpit and charging the parishioners £13,000. In that year too was installed a splendid organ, designed by the firm of Grey & Davidson, who won a major prize for it at the Great Exhibition. The second potential disaster was that in latter years the church and organ had both been allowed to decay, and their restoration has in part been achieved by the LDDC.

Hardwick's Euston station has gone. So, alas, has the splendid classical St Katharine's Dock House which he designed in 1827. The first was destroyed by bureaucratic vandals, the second by Hitler's Luftwaffe.

Left: Nicholas Hawksmoor was a genius, and as this photograph of St Anne's, Limehouse, shows, never content to build a conventional church. The clock was created by the same firm that made Big Ben.

Hawksmoor was not the only early-nineteenth-century church architect to enhance Docklands. Between 1819 and 1821 John Walters was busy supervising the construction, in stucco and yellow stock brick, of St Paul's, Shadwell. An earlier church here had been paid for by Thomas Neale of Shadwell, who leased the land on which it was built from the Dean of St Paul's Cathedral – from which comes the church's own dedication. By 1817 it was in disrepair, and a new church was paid for with money granted by Parliament as a thanks-offering for Napoleon's defeat at the battle of Waterloo.

The enabling act granting £27,000 to rebuild St Paul's specifically stated that of the parish population, which then amounted to 10,000 people, the far greater part consisted of 'labourers in the docks or on the river'. Not surprisingly, in past times this church was dubbed 'the refuge of seamen', not only because many worshipped there but also because 75 sea captains and their wives are interred in its churchyard and the names of 175 sea captains and their wives are inscribed in the parish registers. Here too is an American connection: the mother and grandparents of Thomas Jefferson, third President of the USA, were baptized here. Its organ survived from the earlier church on this site, and was built by Abraham Jordan in 1714.

Another exquisite early-eighteenth-century church, in the conservation area of Rotherhithe, is St Mary the Virgin. Designed by John James, it is built of yellow brick and dressed with stone, its interior supported on Ionic columns. A former church on this site had been irreparably damaged by flooding. To rebuild a medieval church in 1715 indicates the growing wealth of this part of the docklands. Even so, the parishioners begged for 'coal' money. They went so far as to point out that most of them were 'seamen and watermen who venture their lives in fetching those coals from Newcastle which pay for the Rebuilding of the Churches in London'.

These seamen and watermen begged in vain. Their request was refused, but somehow they found the necessary cash themselves. Fascinatingly, they utilized materials from their calling: piers, clad in plaster but essentially created out of ships' masts; and an altar and two ceremonial chairs made from the wood of the 'Fighting *Temeraire*'. Red bricks and white stone quoins characterize this fine dockland workers' church. Launcelot Dowbiggin designed a stone spire which was added in 1739. Fifty years after its consecration the church was equipped with an organ built by the noted John Byfield; it is still intact and renowned, still enclosed in its Corinthian-style case. A plaque records that the master of the *Mayflower*, Christopher Jones, was buried here in 1622. The building sits amid what was once a village, enclosed by its wharf

Left: **St Matthias, Poplar, built by the East India Company in 1654. Despite later renovations, it is a gem.**
Above right: **A ceiling boss in St Matthias.**

and beside the river. Opposite is Peter Hills School, founded in 1613, though the present red-brick building dates from the early eighteenth century and is enlivened by two statues, one of a girl pupil, the other of a boy. And close by stands a pumping station, designed in the 1840s by Isambard Kingdom Brunel to drain the Rotherhithe to Wapping Thames tunnel.

But the oldest church – indeed the oldest surviving building in London Docklands – is St Matthias, Poplar. It began life in 1654 as a chapel for the East India Company. Massive oak columns which once supported its roof were replaced in the next century by stone ones. The building was cruciform, a pattern which appealed to Victorian church architects, but even so in 1866 Milford Teulon, the brother of Samuel Saunders Teulon and an equally bizarre architect, thought fit to add a chancel, clothe the whole building in Kentish ragstone and append what he considered a suitable medieval turret and medieval windows.

Milford Teulon did not, however, much alter the interior of St Matthias. To restore this historic monument to its original appearance was long an aim of the London Docklands Development Corporation, which it finally achieved in 1993.

Poplar also boasts its own splendid parish church, in East India Dock Road. All Saints was designed by Charles Hollis in the early 1820s at a cost of more than £30,000, all raised by the parishioners. Hollis built it in the Greek Revival style, using Ionic capitals for the portico (which is topped by a steeple) and faced it expensively in Portland stone. When you enter you find the Ionic style transformed into the Corinthian style. This was an up-to-date building: the columns inside (unfortunately removed in the 1950s, along with the galleries) were made of cast-iron. This innovative architect also built the brick clergy house opposite. Inside the church is another fine Victorian organ, brought here from a redundant Congregational church. In their work to restore All Saints, Poplar, the authorities in charge have benefited from financial help from the LDDC.

Yellow brick, varied in the mid-Victorian fashion by bands of darker bricks (now visible because the LDDC helped to pay for their cleaning), predominates in the design of St Peter's, which J. F. Pownall built for Wapping in 1866. Though the heyday of Victorian Gothic was approaching, this is still a classical church, with an exceedingly elegant brick spire. Inside, as if to take revenge on this classicism, is a brilliant Gothic rood screen, as well as polychrome brickwork and paintings of angels and saints.

To find a full-blown late-Victorian church you must visit the Isle of Dogs, where in the 1880s F. Johnstone designed a church which was funded by William Cubitt, the

man responsible for developing Cubitt Town on the Isle of Dogs. Brick and stone delineate its spire. And one other church spire deserves a mention, though its church was destroyed in the Second World War, namely the mid-eighteenth-century, onion-domed one that graced St John's, Wapping. It rises close to Wapping Pierhead, where houses built between

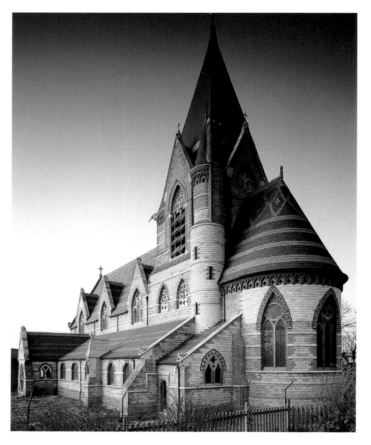

Left: The innovative architect Samuel Saunders Teulon designed St Mark's Church, Silvertown, in the Royal Docks. Built between 1861 and 1862, it is enlivened with polychromatic brickwork.
Right: This tower is a lovely and unique survivor, for after the Second World War, little else remained of Joel Johnson's Church of St John, Wapping.

1811 and 1813 for senior dock officials can still be seen. As for Wapping High Street, in former times no fewer than 36 taverns once graced this riverfront thoroughfare, slaking the thirst of sailors and dockers.

Utterly over-the-top in Victorian architectural excess was St Mark's, Silvertown, by the flamboyant Samuel Saunders Teulon. Stone, brick and ceramics enlivened its interior, until a disastrous fire destroyed much of this

polychromatic masterpiece. The LDDC worked with the local Passmore Edwards Trust to restore it as a museum of Victorian life. But so far this has not been accomplished, and the church is just a store-room.

Church-building in Docklands did not end in the nineteenth century. One superb building, Holy Trinity Church in Jamaica Road, is a masterpiece by the twentieth-century genius H. S. Goodhart-Rendel. He built it after an earlier church was destroyed by Hitler's bombs in 1940. Completed in 1960, this rare gem is modelled on the Romanesque churches of south-west France and boasts stripes of red and blue brick, some of them diagonal, some angled.

Goodhart-Rendel also designed secular buildings, and one of them, St Olaf House in Tooley Street, is an art deco masterpiece. He gave it a steel and gold clock. Across 26 metres (85 feet) of its façade run gold letters spelling 'Hays Wharf'.

Tooley Street is also the home of Hay's Galleria, mid-nineteenth-century warehouses restored to their original appearance on the waterfront but inside transformed in the 1980s into shops, houses and apartments. A magical arch, supported by steel columns, spans the former docks.

Two other churches also recall the heyday of the docks. St Olaf's, in Albion Street, was built for Norwegian seamen in 1927 to the design of John Seaton Dahl, and in those prosperous days it boasted a congregation of 100 worshippers. Olaf is the name of five kings of Norway, and the King of Norway usually visits the church once a year. Fittingly, the copper spire of St Olaf's supports a weathervane in the shape of a Viking longboat. Not far away, and also in Albion Street, stands the modernist, plain (and, it must be said, uninspiring) Finnish seamen's church. Its virtues include a canteen and a reading room.

Opposite:
In Rotherhithe, the stone spire of St Mary the Virgin (added by the architect Lancelot Dowbiggin in the late 1740s) rises above an elegant brick building designed by John James in the second decade of the eighteenth century. *Above:* **A restful scene in Hay's Galleria.**

Not all of Docklands' churches are Scandinavian or Anglican. St Patrick's in Wapping was designed for Catholics, most of them Irish, in 1879, and built of London stock brick, apart from its Portland stone pediment. Inside are massive Ionic columns, which become Corinthian in the chancel. Again the LDDC has contributed to its restoration. And in 1856 the Presbyterians built St Paul's Church on the Isle of Dogs – a polychrome brick building in the Romanesque style (now serving as an arts centre – The Space – with LDDC funding). Its founder was John Scott Russell, whose nearby shipyard was at that time building Isambard Kingdom Brunel's *Great Eastern* with a largely Scottish workforce.

The LDDC has also ventured a little way outside Docklands in supporting the restoration of St James's, Bermondsey, an extremely impressive Waterloo church, built to the plans of James Savage in the late 1820s.

As you ride along Docklands Light Railway, the spires of some of these churches successively reveal themselves. But they are not the only architectural gems situated in Docklands. Recognizing early on that attracting private investment would mean creating an attractive environment, the LDDC has consistently encouraged excellence in the fields of design and construction, with a result that in the last 16 years, Docklands has been the recipient of over 80 awards for design, conservation and landscaping.

It is fair to say that until the late 1970s the existing architecture of Docklands was largely ignored. Consequently, many fine examples of early- and mid-nineteenth-century architecture were demolished, while many of the docks themselves were filled in to create development land. Three vital decisions were made at the outset of the LDDC's development strategy in an attempt to counter the neglect of recent years. Firstly, the dock filling should cease, and the waterside areas' natural advantages as prime sites for housing and leisure developments should be exploited. Secondly, existing buildings, street patterns and open spaces should be retained, and would be key reference points for development planning. No more buildings of any quality would be demolished. Finally, the Corporation would ensure that any developments commissioned by itself, or by developers who had purchased land from the LDDC, set new standards in design and materials.

So conservation went hand in hand with innovative new design. Take Butlers Wharf, for example. When these massive, eight-storey brick warehouses were built in the early 1870s, to the designs of James Tolley, straddling Shad Thames in Bermondsey, this was the largest wharf on the river. The pride of its owners meant that this was no mere shed. Instead it was glamorized with Doric columns. But it was also functional. Bridges between the buildings enabled men trundling barrows to transport goods from the shore to where they could be stored. After a devastating fire, part of the building was not restored but demolished.

Right: A redundant church transformed into an arts centre. Built of stone and polychromatic brick in the Romanesque style, St Paul's Presbyterian Church has a fascinating history. Its architect, Thomas Knightly, was commissioned by the shipbuilder John Scott Russell, who laid the foundation stone in 1856.

outstanding example of urban regeneration? Even so, the place is fascinating. And above it is The Blueprint Café, another enterprise stimulated by Sir Terence Conran. Well designed, with a balcony overlooking Tower Bridge and the towpath, it serves not only visitors but also, and principally, the office workers who find it convenient to walk here.

In fact, most lightermen heartily disliked Butlers Wharf, since at low tide mud frequently immobilized the barges. Men known as 'luters' had to clear the mud with large rakes. Another irritation was that dockers were paid different rates for handling different commodities. The wharf closed down in 1972. The last ships to dock came from East Germany. In 1981, Sir Terence Conran and his architectural practice Conran Roche, put forward restoration proposals for the Butlers Wharf building and five adjacent warehouses, which were actively supported by the LDDC. Today Butlers Wharf flourishes as a series of apartment blocks, enhanced with shops and restaurants. Anchors, ships' chains and propellers add to its ambience.

This is also the site of the Design Museum, the brainchild of Sir Terence Conran. Once an unprepossessing 1950s' warehouse, it is now gleaming white, transformed in the late 1980s and a perfect example of that era of architecture: virginal, displaying much stainless steel and timber floors. Occasionally the white texture of the Design Museum varies, though only into grey, black and blue. It is well worth a visit, not simply for its exhibitions (some of them temporary) and its reference library, but also for its view of the Thames. Its main themes depict the influence of design and technology on our culture and commerce. Yet this remains a curiosity. Why should one need a design museum, with the whole area now an

Another treat on Butlers Wharf is Anchor Brewhouse. 'Brewhouse' refers to the John Courage brewery, which began producing ales here in 1787. As its trade increased, the brewery rebuilt its premises. After John Courage closed down its brewery in 1982, the ten-storey Victorian building was converted into flats and office space. But one can still discern the former tripartite usage: the boilerhouse to the east, its tall chimney still intact; at the centre the old brewhouse, once housing huge copper vats; and beside Tower Bridge the malt mill, where barges once delivered sacks of malt.

Above: The Design Museum on Butlers Wharf, Shad Thames, was completed in 1989. The statue in front, by Eduardo Paolozzi, represents both Isaac Newton and James Watt.

Right: New Concordia Wharf in Bermondsey was converted from a group of late-Victorian warehouses in the 1980s. Meticulous care was taken to preserve the architectural character of the original building; even the 1930s wall cranes were restored.

stanchions black, the walls an almost garish red. One nautical touch is the stern of a boat, named *The Great Harry*, which peeps out from the two central stanchions. This is an impudently brilliant building which, not surprisingly, in 1986 gained an urban design award from the Royal Institute of British Architects and in 1989 a Civic Trust award.

China Wharf is a delightful example of playful yet competent architecture. Piers Gough, who designed it, has gone on record as observing that when in the 1960s, at the age of 16, he was persuaded by his father to become an architect, he judged most modern architecture to be bad and considered that even if he was not very good in the profession, he would be better than most.

When qualified, he produced exciting, flamboyant designs, and the apartments and office block he designed for China Wharf are among the most flamboyant. Wedged between Reed Wharf and New Concordia Wharf, it presents to the former a brick façade that resembles one of the old warehouses. The boldness of Piers Gough's design only reveals itself from the riverside. Four concrete stanchions rising from the water support it. Above, balconies surmounted by arches overlook the Thames. The colour scheme is as audacious as the architecture: the

Left: Piers Gough designed the fanciful China Wharf in the 1980s. It rises impressively from the Thames, with the balconies of its flats overlooking the river.

Above right: Cascades is an architectural jest, its name reflecting its shape. Built in eighteen months between 1986 and 1988, it incorporates 171 apartments of varying sizes, each with splendid Thamesside views.

Piers Gough and his practice Campbell Zogolovitch Wilkinson Gough were also responsible for another, quite bizarre and innovative building in London Docklands. Cascades, on the Isle of Dogs, was completed in 1988. Its name derives from one of its sides, which seems to cascade down to the riverside, while encompassing penthouses, each of which has its own terrace. Here again nautical themes emerge in the architecture of Docklands: portholes for windows as well as simulated ships' bridges and turrets. Once again, different coloured bricks (this time blue and yellow) enhance the design. Since Canary Wharf was to incorporate high-rise buildings, so Cascades was allowed to rise 20 storeys high on London's skyline. Those

fortunate enough to live there have stunning views both of the City of London and of the eastern reaches of the Thames towards Greenwich.

If some find it more or less crazy in design, Cascades is humanized by the City Pride public house at its foot. Next to it rises the Anchorage, a ten-storey residential complex overlooking the river, its walls likewise pierced by portholes. But this building, despite its name, does not derive from a nautical base. The Anchorage rises on the site of Morton House, a soup and canned food factory.

Below: Vaulted
Tobacco Dock, in part
destroyed by bombs
during the Second
World War and
restored as a
shopping village in
the late 1980s by
the Terry Farrell
Partnership.

Close by, across the river in the Surrey
Docks, is another entrancing Docklands
pub, the half-timbered Blacksmith's Arms
(its mock-Tudor front added only in the
1930s). In the past blacksmiths were
vital to the prosperity of the Thames,
and on this site they forged guns for the
Deptford naval yard. This pub has royal
connections. Tsar Peter the Great came
here to study shipbuilding. HRH Queen
Elizabeth the Queen Mother drank here
when gracing the LDDC's 'Downtown'
housing initiative in 1988 – a visit
commemorated in the pub by her portrait.
Dockers used to play a game here called
'Down the Slot', which involved dropping
halfpennies through a hole and betting
on who could drop the most. The proceeds
were given to a local hospital. Today a
brass plate recalls the game. Another
brass plate, recalling the vagaries of the
Thames, marks where the river rose
2 metres (6½ feet) above its predicted
height in January 1928, flooding all the
houses along the riverside – a disaster no
longer possible since the creation of the
Thames Barrier.

The redevelopment of New Concordia
Wharf, though not as spectacular as the
China Wharf development, was of singular
importance for the regeneration of
Docklands. Andrew Wadsworth, the
businessman who bought it in 1980, took

over a mill, a water-tower and some
warehouses which had been built in 1885
to store grain imported mostly from
Concordia, Missouri, in the USA. Less than
a century later, after the warehouses had
been used to store tea, rubber and paper,
they were in a dire condition. Andrew
Wadsworth's architects were commissioned
to provide flats, a roof garden, car parking
(underground), offices and a swimming
pool. They were also briefed not to
transform the warehouses in such a way
that their original function ceased to be
visible to eyes open to once-fine
industrial architecture. Every new window
was to match the old ones. Cast iron was
still to be used for the columns. Its 1930s
cranes – no longer functional – were left
intact, an evocative reminder of the past.

If the final result is a pastiche of late-
nineteenth-century industrial building,
it is a successful one. Again, the
redevelopment was recognized with
awards: a Europa Nostra medal in 1985,
and two years later awards both from the
Times-RICS and the Civic Trust.

Similarly, Tobacco Dock in Wapping now
houses shops where once was stored
tobacco – and, later in its history,
sheepskins and imported furs. Daniel
Asher Alexander designed this dock in
1811, and the building was completed two
years later. Tobacco Dock represents an
early-nineteenth-century architectural
innovation. Alexander utilized the new
iron-casting techniques to support on
cast-iron columns a single-storey
warehouse; its six bays, each with a span
of nearly 16.5 metres (54 feet) and a
clearing of nearly 4 metres (13 feet),
rising from a sophisticated network of
columns and covered by timber roof
trusses. The warehouse came to be known
as the 'Skin Floor', after its usual stock.
Another innovation was Alexander's wine
and spirit cellars, 8 hectares (20 acres)
of brick vaults (supported on granite
pillars) at the base of the building.
In consequence of these superb
nineteenth-century architectural
innovations, Tobacco Dock was declared
a Grade I listed building.

Below: The Circle apartment complex was built on the site of the early-nineteenth-century stables of Courage Brewery, fittingly commemorated by Shirley Pace's statue of a dray horse.

Today the cellar of the Skin Floor hosts shops, interspersed between the vaults and fittingly enlivened by cast-iron window frames, doors and ornamental brackets mimicking Victorian designs. To add to the ambience, a couple of sailing ships, replicas of the eighteenth-century *The Three Sisters* and *The Sea Lark*, are moored at the quayside. The first brought

Left: **Free Trade Wharf, a residential complex created out of a couple of warehouses built for the East India Company to store gunpowder.**
Right: **The impressive dome of Canary Wharf retail complex.**

tobacco from the West Indies, as well as plying elsewhere. Built in Blackwall Yard in 1788, she weighed 330 tonnes. The second was a schooner built in America.

Dating from further back in Docklands' history is the riverside Free Trade Wharf, whose name dates only from 1858 but which was built in Shadwell for the East India Company in 1795. The company used its two warehouses for storing saltpetre, and these warehouses were partly transformed by the architect Richard Jupp in the 1870s. Over the portal you can still see the coat of arms of the East India Company, though Free Trade Wharf is today a development of apartments, with the original building converted into offices and leisure facilities.

The architects who designed these wharves were susceptible to the often dramatic developments of Victorian architecture. In consequence, in Olivers Wharf, Wapping, you unexpectedly discover, next to the baroque tower of what was once St John's Church, that Olivers Wharf itself is a Gothic building.

At Canary Wharf, visitors to Docklands leap into the late twentieth century, though on a spot where once tomatoes from the Canary Islands were unloaded. Its name derives from these Canary Islands, whence in past times came its many other cargoes, unloaded at the West India Docks. Modelled on developments in Manhattan and Toronto and built between 1987 and 1991, Canary Wharf is dominated by a tower designed by the Argentinian-American architect Cesar Pelli, 244 metres (800 feet) high, and topped with a pyramid. As well as housing offices, this complex has a human face, with

supermarkets, fountains, restaurants, wine bars and food shops. Its architects were clever enough to cope with the winds that such high-rise buildings can cause: from time to time, when the winds are excessive, the fountain in Cabot Square is turned off by a device which sits on top of one of the lamps and spins in the wind.

Canary Wharf has distinct architectural components. This unfocused but beguiling group of buildings begins with Westferry Circus, tree-lined, laid out by Hanna Olins, its gates and railings (designed by Giuseppe Lund) symbolizing the four seasons. Westferry Circus leads onto Pelli's pyramid-topped tower and around this impressive edifice rise a mixture of buildings of eclectic styles, including 1 Cabot Square (designed by I. M. Pei, Harry Cobb, Freed and Partners); 10 Cabot Square (by the Chicago firm of Skidmore, Owens and Merrill); 20 Cabot Square and 30 South Colonnade (by Kohn Pederson Fox Architects); and 25 North Colonnade (by John Troughton and Jamie McAslan). Work on the fine shopping centre at Canary Wharf was carried out by the British Building Design Partnership.

And the great river also has made its own mark on Docklands' architecture. The water-pumping stations are not mere functional buildings but pieces of architectural fantasy. In Newham the engineer Sir Joseph Bazalgette designed the Abbey Mills Pumping Station in a resplendent Gothic style in 1868.

Below and right: **Storm Water Pumping Station, John Outram's entertainingly bizarre building, won a Civic Trust award in 1989, and adds a kaleidoscope of colour to the Isle of Dogs.**

This playful tradition continues. John Outram designed the Storm Water Pumping Station on the Isle of Dogs in the 1980s and gave it Chinese-style eaves, a fan like the engine of a jet plane and a roof of green glazed tiles. He used red, yellow and blue-grey bricks for the walls (the blue-grey ones to mirror the colour of the Thames). There are no windows. Somewhat arcanely, Outram declared, 'The building proposes that there are some things, like the rain, that we must now plan and calculate to preserve as they are today, for ever.' In spite of this virtually incomprehensible architect's talk, the building is a success. In 1989 his pumping station won a Civic Trust award.

Another Docklands pumping station is the work of the Richard Rogers Partnership. Tidal Basin Pumping Station in the Royal Docks (at the north-west corner of Royal Victoria Dock), like John Outram's pumping station, deploys children's paint-box primary colours – red for its doors, yellow for its walkways, blue for much of the rest. A couple of concentric drums crown the building. Its purpose is to lift waste water from underground channels and pour it back into the River Thames.

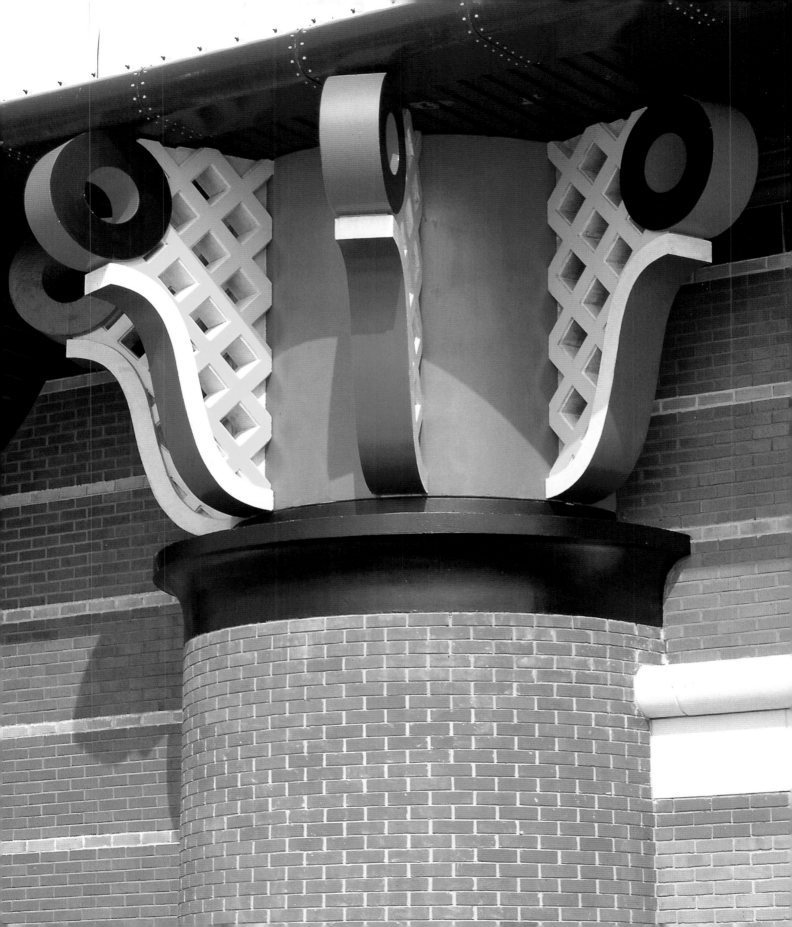

Surrey Docks is another part of East London transformed from decline to new life by the LDDC. After the closure of the docks in 1968, the Port of London Authority and the London Borough of Southwark set about filling in most of them. The council began working on new roads and some landscaping of the area. Warehouses were torn down. By the end of 1981 when land on the Surrey Docks peninsula was vested in the new London Docklands Development Corporation, Surrey Quays and Greenland Dock were ripe for regeneration. An ecological park comprising nearly 3 hectares (7½ acres) of land was established. A watersports centre was opened at Greenland Dock, and a yacht marina in South Dock.

Stimulated by the LDDC, nearly 5,000 dwellings were completed here. Not all of them were new – some were refurbished or converted. Riverside walkways were created, as well as green open spaces (the finest being Lavender Pond) and nature reserves. Dock walls were repaired. Trees were planted: plane trees, cherries, eucalypti, Italian alders. Granite setts were laid. Towards the end of 1988 a comprehensive shopping centre was opened next to Canada Water. A new canal was dug, to link Surrey Water and Canada Water. Associated Newspapers, publishers of the *Daily Mail* and the *London Evening Standard*, set up a major printing works at Surrey Quays.

Newspapers played a major role in transforming the image of Docklands. As their headquarters moved into the Urban Development Area, so perceptions about it changed. And these newspapers believed in housing their staff in fine buildings. In the same decade as the *Daily Mirror*

moved into Docklands, Nicholas Grimshaw designed a splendid Docklands printing plant for the *Financial Times*, with two glass walls, massive blue printing presses, aluminium cladding and an exterior lift with staircase towers. This is a most bizarre yet delightful building, whose massive blue printing presses could be viewed by startled motorists as they drove by. Sadly, the presses are no more, the victim of overcapacity in the printing industry.

Docklands' architects have long been fond of their logos. At Plaistow Wharf in the late 1940s Tate & Lyle built an impressive new warehouse, clad in Portland stone. Mindful of the biblical legend, 'Out of the

strong came sweetness', the architects decorated the building with a lion and bees. Tate & Co. had set up a factory at Silvertown in 1871. Ten years later Lyle & Sons began their business. They imported sugar cane from the West Indies and south east Africa. Tate merged with Lyle in 1921. Until 1979 they boasted their own fleet of ships, Sugar Line Ltd. These sugar refiners were philanthropic. For their employees they created a small, exquisite stretch of green land, Lyle Park, on the river in what is now the Borough of Newham.

Yet more surreal is the Thames Barrier, silver and huge, reminiscent of Sydney Opera House but designed to protect London from rare but potentially lethal high tides. Work began in 1975 and was finished in 1982, at a cost of £435 million. The barrier stretches 520 metres (1,706 feet) across the river, and has ten shipping gates – four major ones, six smaller ones. Each of the major ones weighs some 3,000 tonnes. Separating the gates are massive concrete piers, on which rise the stainless-steel-clad buildings that house the hydraulic machinery. The gates are pivoted; they open and close by turning through 90 degrees. When open, they lie on concrete on the river bed, to enable shipping to pass over them.
To enhance this part of Docklands, in 1995 the LDDC launched an international competition to select a landscape artist who would design an 8.8-hectare (22-acre) riverside park on land adjacent to the Barrier.

These are the more spectacular elements that make up the architecture of Docklands. But no one should neglect to glimpse some of its innovative housing estates. Cubitt Town is among the most noteworthy. It was begun in the early 1840s. Brick fields, a pottery, a cement factory and timber wharves were worked by the families (mostly Irish) who lived on this housing estate.

Providing homes for Docklands' citizens has been a major part of the LDDC's remit. Just over 39,000 people lived here in 1981. By 1997 the number had risen to

Below: A piquant reminder of the past: redundant cranes tower above the modern West Silvertown Urban Village.

Right: One of the modern wonders of the world: the gleaming Thames Barrier, both a triumph of engineering and science and a masterpiece of industrial architecture.

80,000. While the need to promote land for housing was pressing, the LDDC saw that it was equally vital that any future housing developments achieved a high standard of design. Directly commissioning outline designs for some of its key sites from leading firms of architects, including Richard McCormack, Darbourne & Dark and Jeremy Dixon, set the standard which the Corporation encouraged house builders to follow. A panel of eminent architects and other designers with an interest in the urban environment were also appointed to advise the LDDC on design matters, meeting on a regular basis throughout the year to consider key projects such as the West Silvertown Urban Village.

In describing the architecture and design of Docklands, it is an error to forget that often these ancient and modern buildings combine delightfully, sometimes in breathtaking ensembles. By 1981, when the LDDC was set up, the boroughs of Tower Hamlets and Southwark had already designated ten such areas as outstanding.

These were the Tower conservation area, Wapping Pierhead conservation area, St Anne's Church conservation area, Narrow Street conservation area in Limehouse, Coldharbour conservation area and Island Gardens conservation area (both on the Isle of Dogs), St Saviour's Dock conservation area, Tower Bridge conservation area, Alfred Salter conservation area and St Mary's, Rotherhithe conservation area.

Each has its own special delights. The Alfred Salter conservation area is particularly fascinating. Bermondsey Borough Council built it between 1924 and 1929, inspired by the visionary local doctor and MP Alfred Salter. This was one of London's earliest so-called 'garden villages'; its houses were designed as cottages. To the north is Cherry Garden Pier, where once cherries did grow. Close by rise King's Garden Stairs, named after Edward III, who would climb them to reach his manor house. Happily, remains of the manor house itself were discovered in 1983 and have been excavated (at a cost to the LDDC of £700,000), to be preserved as an historic landmark of this part of Docklands.

Left: **Buy a pint and imbibe the past. The Angel is a pub and restaurant built in the 1850s, but its origins are more remote: the first record of an inn with this name on this spot occurs in 1682.**

Another asset is the Angel public house, close by Cherry Garden Pier and blessed with marvellous views of the Thames and the lower pool of London. Though the present pub, with its evocative oak beams, panelling and pillars, dates from the mid-nineteenth century, it derives from a rest-house, founded in the fifteenth century (if not before), where the monks of Bermondsey Priory cared for travellers, to whom they would serve beer. Its present name derives from the lord of the manor, William Angell.

We know that Samuel Pepys stayed here, buying cherries for his wife from the cherry garden. Smugglers relished its strategic position. Here also Captain Cook stayed, while planning his 1768 voyage to Australia and New Zealand. It was here too that the painter J. M. W. Turner watched the 'Fighting *Temeraire*' being towed for breaking up and painted one of his most celebrated works, in which he depicted the doomed vessel.

Narrow Street conservation area, stretching from Limekiln Dock (whose waterfront is defined by Emery Street) to the Regent's Canal Dock, retains warehouses and The Grapes, a celebrated pub overlooking the river. Wapping Pierhead conservation area once embraced two noble churches, but the late-eighteenth-century St John's was mostly demolished in the Second World War and only its tower remains. The Roman Catholic church of St Patrick, built in 1879, is still intact, its marble altar a

Below: First known as The Shippe, The Mayflower got its present, illustrious name after beams from the famous pilgrim vessel were incorporated into the building.

marvel of Victorian Gothic. Georgian houses, built for dock officials by Daniel Alexander in the second decade of the nineteenth century, have been transformed into luxurious homes. So have warehouses fronting the river. Another development west of Wapping Pierhead has seen Black Eagle Wharf (so named after the black eagle logo of Truman's beer, whose casks were once handled here) become similarly lavish homes.

Coldharbour conservation area protects nineteenth-century houses built for officials of the West India Dock Company. Situated on the east of the Isle of Dogs, it embraces the eastern entrance of the West India and Millwall Docks. For tourists its chief attraction may well be the Gun public house, so named after the first ship to enter West India Import Dock in 1802, which fired her guns (or perhaps because gunsmiths lived and worked nearby in earlier times). The publican will show visitors a peephole through which smugglers would watch for customs officers. Even more intriguing is the legend that when Horatio Nelson stayed here Emma Hamilton, living nearby, would visit him through an underground passage.

Tall warehouses, transformed into homes and offices, characterize St Saviour's Dock conservation area at Butlers Wharf – warehouses which once stored tea and spice. Even more delightful is the conservation area of St Mary's, Rotherhithe. Its chief attraction, of course, is the church, built in 1715. But there are also other treats. One is The Mayflower public house. From its jetty in 1620 the Pilgrim Fathers embarked in their ship the *Mayflower* for Plymouth and then America. A pub has stood here certainly from the mid-sixteenth century, and was once named The Shippe, and the present building has beams from the Pilgrim Fathers' own vessel. As for other

fascinating architecture of this conservation area, the early-nineteenth-century brick façades of Thames Tunnel Mills, once a flour warehouse, now front flats, though reminders of past times are the silo tower and the free-standing chimney, 24 metres (79 feet) high.

St Anne's Church conservation area, Limehouse, surrounds an entrancing early-eighteenth-century church, while the Tower conservation area is blessed with warehouses designed by the distinguished early-nineteenth-century architect Philip Hardwick and by docks built by the brilliant engineer Thomas Telford. Tower Bridge conservation area is by contrast a haven of Victorian building.

To these conservation areas the LDDC added seven more: Wapping Wall conservation area, St Paul's Church conservation area in Shadwell, West India Dock conservation area, Chapel House conservation area on the Isle of Dogs, St Matthias conservation area, All Saints' conservation area (both in Poplar) and Naval Row conservation area at East India Dock.

Below: St Saviour's
Dock today
encompasses some of
the most innovative
architecture of
London Docklands,
its elongated
warehouses restored
as homes and offices.

163

Wapping Wall conservation area is a honeypot for devotees of urban architecture, comprising a slender, walled High Street which runs from Shadwell Basin to Wapping Pierhead, and encompassing eighteenth-century terraced houses and warehouses. The Georgian houses of Wapping Pierhead, built for top officials of the docks, have been matched by houses built by the borough of Tower Hamlets. Olivers Wharf, on Wapping High Street, is a Victorian Gothic warehouse now converted into flats. Since Ramsgate fishermen landed their catches at Wapping Old Stairs, the local pub is reasonably called The Town of Ramsgate. Originally, however, it was known as The Red Cow, and even before that, from its foundation in the 1460s, as The Hostel. Captured pirates were regularly drowned at Wapping Old Stairs. Here too mariners would return to be reunited with their wives and sweethearts, reunions commemorated by a rhyming couplet on a wall in the pub:

Your Polly has never been faithless she
    swears,
Since last time we parted at Wapping
    Old Stairs.

St Paul's Church conservation area is small and exquisite; steps take you down from the churchyard to Shadwell Basin, with its sports centre (for canoeing and sailing), an old dock wall separating the area from The Highway, and the modern sand-coloured and brick houses flanking three sides of the dock.

West India Dock conservation area boasts a row of dock constables' houses, which were built by John Rennie in 1819, the middle one to house the police sergeant, the outer pair to house his subordinates. In Hertsmere Road stands the superb former Dockmaster's House, which was designed in 1807 by Thomas Morris, engineer to the West India Dock Company. This part of Docklands is graced with the Cannon Workshops, which were built in the mid-1820s by Sir John Rennie, and at West India Quay by two magical neo-classical warehouses (all that remain of the nine that survived the Second World War) built in brick by George Gwilt of Southwark 20 years earlier. In 1803 Gwilt also designed the Ledger Building on the north quay of the West India Import Dock, a building whose portico resembles a Greek temple.

At one stage the LDDC found this a useful as well as handsome site for its administration offices, though the Ledger Building's original purpose was to shelter records of rum, sugar, timber, grain and general cargoes. A moat defended the perimeter of the West India Docks, and its gate piers of 1802 still survive. Another building redolent of past times is the early-twentieth-century Salvation Army Hostel, designed in the Queen Anne style by Niven and Wigglesworth. The Salvation Army took over this hostel only in the 1930s, for it was first designated as a temperance house for sailors – particularly Scandinavians, hence its inauguration in 1902 by the Swedish Ambassador.

Right: In 1811, building on behalf of senior dock officials, David Asher Alexander was the architect of these

Georgian terraces at Wapping Pierhead. Following conversion in the 1970s, they are today prized homes.

Chapel House conservation area was an innovative conglomeration of three estates built by Poplar Borough Council after the First World War, under the influence of the 'garden city' dream. Red-brick cottages are set in a pleasant environment, some of them sheltered by trees. Terraced dockers' cottages still survive in Cahir Street, and a viaduct built in 1872 still carries the railway (today the Docklands Light Railway) beside Millwall Park.

As you ride to Beckton on the Docklands Light Railway you pass a remarkable brick building created in 1857 for the East India Dock Company. This was once a hydraulic pumping station, and is the chief delight of the Naval Row conservation area. The old dock wall still protects this part of Docklands, the wall itself now being protected by the LDDC.

And for the first time natural reed beds were recreated on a riverbank in Inner London when the Corporation joined forces in 1995 with the National Rivers Association on an ecological initiative to clean up a tidal tributary of the Thames, the River Lea. Large baskets of reeds were planted into silt at low tide, with the intention not only of purifying the river

but also of attracting more fish and bird life. This project complemented nearby Bow Creek, already under development by the LDDC as an urban wetland ecology park. In addition, rare plants had been discovered in this hitherto little-known spot.

In these conservation areas, parks and wharves, churches and warehouses, basins and docks, pubs and quiet streets all add to the ambience, with the River Thames never far away.

Left: **Since 1989, Shadwell Basin has been surrounded on three sides by elegant, sand-coloured homes, with arcades, arches and porthole windows.** *Above right:* **Royal Victoria Dock.**

Travelling in Docklands

6

‘How far is it to Bethlehem?’

‘Not very far.’

Frances Chesterton

Opposite: **New thoroughfares, both road and rail, are the arteries of the regenerated Docklands.**

Frances Chesterton's poem is almost apposite for those travelling to Docklands, though of course she was writing about the birthplace of Jesus. But just south of Docklands, in Southwark, was once situated the city's most notorious hospital for the insane, founded in 1247 on behalf of the Sheriff of London as a priory of the order of the Star of Jerusalem – named after the star which led the Magi to the birthplace of Jesus. However, most people called it not Bethlehem but Bedlam. Bethlehem Hospital was for many years not even as hospitable as the stable in which Jesus was born. Long treated as a sort of theatre, where curious spectators would come to view the demented inmates, it was portrayed most memorably in the eighth of William Hogarth's engravings of *The Rake's Progress*.

And, from Southwark, as indeed from the heart of London, the Docklands are not very far. They also used to live up to the vision of another poet, William Wordsworth:

... silent, bare,
Ships, towers, domes, theatres, and
   temples lie
Open unto the fields, and to the sky,
All bright and glittering in the smokeless
   air.

Right: **Four sailing ships, berthed in 1898 in the Regent's Canal Dock; the** *Napoli* **and three Norwegian vessels, the** *Vale*, **the** *Albion* **and the** *Dusty Miller*. **The Norwegian ships carried cargoes of cod-oil, dried cod and wood.**

Later it became smokier. When Charles Dickens wrote (in *Bleak House*) of fog, he described fog up the river, 'where it flows among green straits and meadows'. He also described fog down the river, 'where it rolls defiled, among the tiers of shipping, and the waterside pollutions of a great (and dirty) city'. Even earlier, when Joel Johnson designed St John's Church in Wapping High Street, he built it of dark brick, contrasting with white stone, in the hope that it would still be recognized through the mists.

Today the London pea-souper fogs have gone, but so have most of the ships. There still are some vessels sailing the river, but they are few compared with those of yester-year. The losses in Docklands include speedy and convenient passenger ferries.

As early as the fifteenth century, small, fast ships, known as carvels, some with two masts, others with three, were sailing up the Thames with merchandise bound for the port of London. Dutch vessels, among the most advanced of the sixteenth and seventeenth centuries, also arrived, and were admired and later copied by those who constructed Thames barges. People were used to travelling by water.

NAPOLI. BERGEN

In the early nineteenth century paddle steamers greatly improved transport not only on the Thames but on other major British rivers. Such a service between Woolwich, Greenwich and London was set up in the mid-1830s, dropping people off at piers *en route*. Eventually, four times in an hour passengers could expect the arrival of such steamers, run by rival companies, the City Steamboat Company and the General Steam Navigation Company, which also took passengers as far as the Kent and Essex seaside towns. Some of their ferries even had first- and second-class cabins.

Increasingly suffering from competition by the railways, the companies joined forces in 1865. They struggled on, generating less and less profit, before finally giving up the ghost in 1902. Alarmed, London County Council decided to run its own service, commissioning 30 new steamers. This venture proved disastrously unprofitable, and the steamers were sold in 1907. One company which bought some of them managed to continue a summer service, but only till 1914.

Yet the opportunity for running a ferry service remained, and in 1938 river-buses began regularly taking passengers from Greenwich to Westminster and back. After the war passenger ferries continued to run as far as Greenwich. Ten attempts were made to develop the idea, the most ambitious in 1951, when several companies united to found a water-bus service during the Festival of Britain. The scheme collapsed when the Festival ended.

In Victorian times horse-drawn omnibuses transported people from the centre of the city to Woolwich and Greenwich. Their name derived from their French inventor, a Monsieur Omnès of Nantes, who had taken as his motto a Latin pun on his name: *Omnes omnibus* ('All for everyone'). In London they were initially run by George Shillibeer, a London coachbuilder who had worked in Paris and spotted their value there. His business collapsed when the Greenwich railway opened. But buses were here to stay, their number expanded by horse-drawn trams, then by electrified tramcars and trolley-buses. The last tram ran in Docklands in 1952, the last trolley-bus in 1960.

Above: East India Dock Road in 1906. On the right is the former entrance to the dock, demolished in 1958 in order not to obstruct the construction of the Blackwall Tunnel. *Right:* In 1964 a Port of London Authority tug tows the Cunard Line *Samaria* into Royal Albert Dock.

Below: Looking west
from the Woolwich
Ferry.

Far right: A flag
proudly announces
the entrance to the
Regent's Canal Dock,
which connects the
Thames with the
canal and was
opened in 1820.

In addition, canals could ease travelling through the area, though not always. The Isle of Dogs Canal was a failure. Its aim was to facilitate cargoes between Limehouse and Wapping, but unfortunately the tugs, their paddles driven by steam, set up such a wash that the banks of the canal were continually damaged. The West India Dock Company

Some parts of Docklands were readily reached, by these and other means. On the north bank of the Thames, Blackwall, for example, was easily accessible from the City of London by way of Poplar and Ratcliff, a route which avoided the tiresome river detour around the Isle of Dogs. Wapping High Street had been constructed in the late sixteenth century. Among its amenities were 36 public houses, usually crammed with sailors. A major deficiency was that only one vehicle at a time could use the street, until the Metropolitan Board of Works decided to widen it in 1879.

The laying out of Commercial Road also helped. The Commercial Road Company built it at the beginning of the nineteenth century for transporting goods to the city from East and West India Docks. Initially this road finished at Black Church Lane, but the Metropolitan Board of Works, a body established in 1855, carried it on to Whitechapel High Street in 1870. In the meantime East India Dock Road, finished in 1810, connected with Commercial Road at Limehouse, so that another straight run into London had been created, this one avoiding Poplar High Street. West India Dock Road was created in the same year, connecting West India Docks to Commercial Road.

ENTRANCE TO THE REGENT'S CANAL, LIMEHOUSE,

decided to cut the losses caused by the continual repairs, and transformed the canal into the South West India Dock.

Three years after the opening of the West India Docks, the City Canal was dug, to make an easy passage across the Isle of Dogs between Blackwall and Wapping. Although there were locks at each end of the canal, no one charged ships for using the canal. It therefore made no profit and was sold in 1829 to the West India Dock Company, which transformed the canal into a dock for its timber trade.

The Limehouse Cut, 2.4 kilometres (1½ miles) long, runs south-west from the Lee Navigation (which starts in Hertford) to join the Regent's Canal. It thus helped to connect London's docklands with the Midlands, for the Regent's Canal, opened in 1812, connects at Paddington Basin with the Grand Junction Canal. The Regent's Canal and Dock Company built a dock at Limehouse with 4 hectares (10 acres) of water and 1.6 hectares (4 acres) of quays and wharves, which closed down only in 1969.

Tunnels also eased the problems of traffic in Docklands. The first, a double tunnel 336 metres (1,200 feet) long, was built by Isambard Kingdom Brunel to connect Rotherhithe and Wapping. It opened in 1843 as a thoroughfare, but was later converted into a railway line.

This Thames Tunnel had long been contemplated. In 1802 a Cornish mining engineer, Robert Vaize (whose nickname was 'the Mole'), offered the first plan for such a tunnel. Three years later the Thames Archway Company was given permission to construct it. The first shaft was sunk at Rotherhithe. In 1807 Richard Trevithick, who had already built the first passenger-carrying steam train and the first locomotive with smooth wheels running on smooth rails, took over from 'the Mole'. He managed to dig a tunnel for around 300 metres (1,000 feet), but then the walls collapsed, the river inundated the work and the project was abandoned.

The idea, however, fascinated Marc Brunel, who in 1818 patented his own tunnelling shield, a device which would allow the least possible excavated tunnel to be revealed while work was in progress, in order to minimize the risk that the sides would collapse. Twelve cast-iron frames supported boards, which were removed only to allow the excavation of 11.5 cm (4½ inches) of soil.

Five years later Marc Brunel gained parliamentary authorization for another attempt to construct a Thames tunnel. His tunnelling shield was not entirely successful, for the walls caved in five times under pressure of the water. In 1827, just before the first of these calamities, Marc's son, Isambard Kingdom, had taken over responsibility for the work. Funds at times ran out – and the work was entirely stopped between 1828 and 1835. The Thames was at that time so polluted that workmen fell ill and died. Eventually Parliament stepped in with financial help, though not enough to pay for ramps for carriages, so that for some 20 years this first Thames Tunnel between Rotherhithe and Wapping was only used by pedestrians. Eventually, in 1869, the East London Railway seized the opportunity to lay a track through it in order to make a cross-river route from New Cross to Shoreditch.

The next Rotherhithe tunnel, connecting Shadwell with Rotherhithe, was designed in the first decade of the twentieth century by Sir Maurice Fitzmarice and stretches for 1,481 metres (4,860 feet). Since large ships passed over it, Sir Maurice put its top 14.5 metres (48 feet) below Trinity High Water. This tunnel delighted some, but not the 3,000 people whose houses were demolished because of related street widening.

Lined with segments of cast-iron, the earlier northbound Blackwall Tunnel was built in the 1890s under the direction of Sir Alexander Binnie. It was 1,344 metres (4,410 feet) long, with an internal diameter of 7.3 metres (24 feet). Its sister tunnel, the southbound one, was built in the 1960s. Finished in 1969, it is 875 metres (2,870 feet) long, with an internal diameter of 8.4 metres (27½ feet).

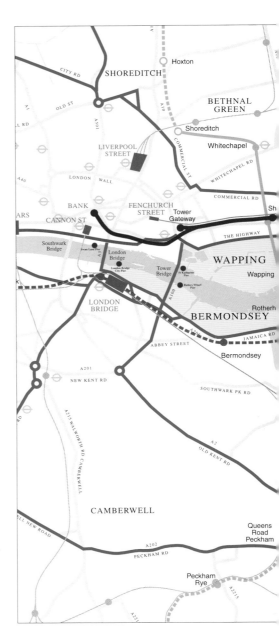

Below: New and improved road and rail links have made accessible a part of London once considered too remote to reach.

177

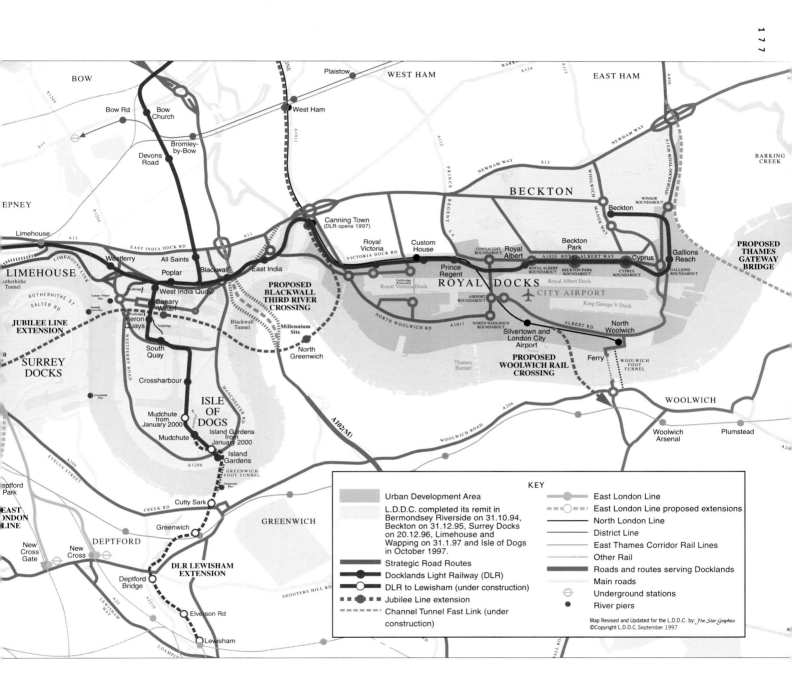

KEY

Urban Development Area

L.D.D.C. completed its remit in Bermondsey Riverside on 31.10.94, Beckton on 31.12.95, Surrey Docks on 20.12.96, Limehouse and Wapping on 31.1.97 and Isle of Dogs in October 1997.

Strategic Road Routes

Docklands Light Railway (DLR)

DLR to Lewisham (under construction)

Jubilee Line extension

Channel Tunnel Fast Link (under construction)

East London Line

East London Line proposed extensions

North London Line

District Line

East Thames Corridor Rail Lines

Other Rail

Roads and routes serving Docklands

Main roads

Underground stations

River piers

Map Revised and Updated for the L.D.D.C. by: *Five Star Graphics*
©Copyright L.D.D.C. September 1997

Sir Alexander Binnie was also responsible for the design of the Greenwich foot tunnel, built between 1897 and 1902. Its internal diameter is 3.3 metres (11 feet), for it was meant as a pedestrian tunnel, its length 371 metres (1,217 feet), as it burrows under the Thames from Greenwich to the Isle of Dogs. It replaced a ferry service that had existed since 1676. (Greenwich seems to have been an important place even in Roman times, for it was served by a Roman road which passed through what is now Greenwich Park.)

In 1834 the first London railway opened, connecting London Bridge with Greenwich, running along a continuous viaduct. It proved so popular that after two years the railway was extended as far as Deptford. By the mid-1830s trains to Woolwich were achieving speeds of 29 kilometres per hour (18 mph). The Blackwall railway, built in the early 1840s, connected Blackwall with Fenchurch Street, for a time had a five-foot gauge and also ran on a viaduct. Unlike its predecessor, it carried goods as well as passengers.

Soon the docks themselves were investing in such railways. The East and West India Docks and Birmingham Junction Railway was authorized by Parliament in 1853, one of its aims being to link the suburbs of

Below: The Royal
Docks, seen from
above Albert Basin.
On the left is King
George V Dock, on
the right Royal
Albert Dock. They
flank London City
Airport, beyond
which stretches Royal
Victoria Dock.

1 7 9

West London to the docks. In the 1860s the Millwall Freehold Land and Dock Company built another railway line, which ran through the West India Docks to connect with the Blackwall Railway. In its early years the owners were so anxious about fire hazards that the trains were pulled not by steam engines but by horses.

When the Royal Victoria Dock opened, four miles from the City, the railways were a boon. Branches of the Great Eastern Railway also flanked both sides of the Royal Albert Dock. Short branch lines connected their tracks with wharves. By the end of the nineteenth century the North Woolwich line was serving not only the Royal Albert Dock but also the gasworks at Beckton.

So repeatedly the transport pattern here was one of boom and decline, matching the rest of the life of the area. With the decline in population in the area, with its increasing unemployment and the consequent relative poverty of its population, with the closure of the docks, with the area's perceived unattractiveness, few were willing to invest in new roads and transport. Successive governments expressed their concern, and in January 1974 Parliament set up a Docklands Joint Committee, charged with drawing up a strategic plan for the area, including transport. Its proposals were for an underground railway link, two major road links and an East London river crossing.

By 1980 little progress had been made and the docks were still closing down. Although physically close to the centre of London, the winding of the Thames with the resulting peninsulas, and the lack of any good road or rail connections, reinforced the perception that Docklands was far removed from the heart of the capital. If investors, home buyers, tenants

and employees were to be attracted to the area, it had to be made accessible by road and rail.

First, the LDDC built a series of red-brick roads to improve accessibility in and around the Isle of Dogs Enterprise Zone. Next the Docklands Clipper, a shuttle bus which ran between Mile End tube station

and the Isle of Dogs, was set up in January 1984, but closed down five years later when the Docklands Light Railway was making it increasingly redundant. By that time the service was providing clippers at five-minute intervals and carrying some 12,000 passengers a week.

Yet as Alan Pearsall, a historian at the National Maritime Museum, rightly wrote in 1986, 'Looking into the future, transport is essential for the rehabilitation of the area.' Speed, frequency and reliability were vital, he said. With new roads, railways and underground lines, the astute architectural historian Stephanie Williams observed in 1990 that the focus of London must move east. By this time the London Docklands Development Corporation had already been at work for nearly a decade.

Above and right:
Reliable bus services and the Docklands Light Railway enhance the quality of life for residents – as do traditional leisure pursuits.

Undoubtedly Canary Wharf eased the problems of creating new links between the centre of London and Docklands. Olympia & York agreed with the LDDC in 1987 that the new commercial centre there should cover over 1.1 million square metres (12 million square feet). The proposals envisaged that Canary Wharf would stimulate an increase in the local workforce by 38,000 people, an estimate enormously boosted in later years. To transport many of these people, it became imperative to hasten the expansion of the Docklands Light Railway.

The DLR's construction had begun in 1984, and it opened in 1987 – a light rail system, driverless, controlled by computers. It was built jointly by John Mowlem plc and the General Electric Company on behalf of London Regional Transport, half its investment of £77 million partly contributed by the LDDC. (With hindsight, one might criticize this initial investment as inadequate, but it seemed sufficient at the time.) Its designers followed the preferred remit of the LDDC, for a futuristic image and a highly visible railway.

The DLR ran and runs both on new tracks and on the old Limehouse and Millwall Viaducts. Initially it ran for 12 kilometres (7½ miles) to link Tower Bridge with the Isle of Dogs and Stratford. This too was initially almost a disaster. Its computer system was inadequate. Her Majesty the Queen opened it, then it was shut down, while the computer system was re-evaluated. Starting up again, the DLR was scarcely able to cope with demand, and even less reliable when its Bank extension, stretching a further 1.5 kilometres (1 mile) to the heart of the City, opened in 1991. Services were erratic and its users understandably displeased.

The following year its ownership was transferred from London Transport to the LDDC, with the remit that reliability must be improved. An extension to Beckton was built and opened two years later. Yet the DLR became in the end one of the most imaginative and successful of all Docklands ventures. A new fleet of trains had been purchased, one-car trains replaced by two-car trains. Platforms had been lengthened, viaducts strengthened, and the railway began to run at 98 per cent reliability. It is also friendly to the physically disabled, who can reach its high-level platforms via lifts and enter the trains on wheelchairs.

Left: **Docklands Light Railway snakes its way through the major development east of the City.**

By 1997 the Docklands Light Railway was carrying up to 70,000 passengers a day, over a system stretching for 21.7 kilometres (13½ miles). An extension as far as Greenwich and Lewisham (which will be completed in January 2000 and provide access to the Millennium Experience site) was necessary to open up the area to the south to local people, and to give access to the Isle of Dogs for some 500,000 residents of south London, and rail commuters from Kent. As part of this DLR Lewisham extension, a major river crossing will also have been completed by early 2000 – for without such crossings the Thames becomes not an asset to east London but a barrier.

In 1988 the LDDC gave its support to the RiverBus service, the aim of which was to sail residents, as well as those who did business in Docklands, between the piers of new developments at Chelsea Harbour in West London and Canary Wharf.

Fares were high, but so was the standard of service. With generous staffing, these eight catamarans had a mere 62 seats. But the vessels were too small to generate a profit. Nor were there enough of them to guarantee a reasonably frequent service, so passengers could not rely on them. Other Thames users complained that the wash from the catamarans was damaging their craft, and the RiverBus vessels were forced to slow down. To add to their problems, some of them were damaged by debris in the Thames.

So by the end of its first year of operation, the RiverBus service was financially stretched. The government of the day offered a rescue grant of £500,000, and five Docklands' developers, one of them Olympia & York of Canary Wharf, promised to support the service for the next four years. By 1992 nearly three-quarters of a million passengers were using the RiverBus.

Then Olympia & York went into administration. Despite desperately seeking funding from other bodies (including local government), RiverBus itself went into administration in August 1993. Undoubtedly one reason was that travelling on it cost more than twice the fare charged for the same journey by bus or rail. Another was an old complaint –

Left: Crossharbour DLR station
Right: Some of the most innovative architecture in Docklands can be seen at its stations: this superbly elegant structure is at Canary Wharf.

competition from the railways, particularly the increasingly successful Docklands Light Railway. A third was that London Transport refused to allow the RiverBus to join the highly successful Travelcard scheme, which integrated bus and rail services in the capital – not unreasonably in view of the higher fares charged by the RiverBus, which would have required London Transport to subsidize the service. A fourth reason was that tourism is seasonal. And finally, the LDDC's Limehouse Link Tunnel had opened to traffic in May 1993, dramatically cutting the drive time between the Isle of Dogs and the City, and exploding the myth that Docklands was difficult to get to.

The liquidators sold eight catamarans to a Bangkok company which now makes use of them for its own tourists. A more modest service now operates into Canary Wharf.

In 1987 Docklands saw the opening of the first new British airport for 40 years, a £30 million project designed to serve the City and London businesses. Its airstrip, at first a mere 762 metres (2,500 feet) in length, was designed to cater for aircraft adapted for short take-off and landing, initially 50-seater four-engined turbo-prop planes. Its 36-hectare (89-acre) site was that of a disused quay between the Royal Albert and King George V Docks. It faced east–west and therefore – particularly from the point of view of air-traffic controllers – was properly aligned with Luton, Gatwick and Heathrow.

London City Airport was a favoured project of the then Chief Executive of the LDDC, Reg Ward, for he saw it as one way of altering people's persisting view of Docklands as an outmoded relic of decline. But many local residents opposed the idea, on the grounds of noise, safety, air pollution and the fact that, once taken up by the airport, the land could not be used for another desirable development. After a public inquiry which lasted for four months, the Secretary of State for the Environment agreed that construction of London City Airport should go ahead.

Such was demand that soon a second public inquiry decided that in spite of the possible increase in noise levels, the business of Docklands and the City required more European capitals to be reached from here, and thus that the runway could be increased to 1,200 metres (3,937 feet), and larger, faster airplanes should be allowed to arrive and take off.

Meanwhile business men and women were already finding that they could quickly reach Amsterdam, Antwerp, Berne, Brussels, Dublin, Düsseldorf, Edinburgh, Frankfurt, Geneva, Lugano, Malmö, Milan, Paris, Rome, Rotterdam, Stockholm, Turin and Zurich from London City Airport. Equally attractive to these customers was the speed at which they could arrive and board a plane – virtually walking into the

Above: **HRH Prince Charles unveils a plaque signalling the inauguration of the building of London City Airport.**

Right: **The airport's planes speed travellers to the major business centres in Europe. An added bonus is that the airport has an amazingly short check-in time.**

airport and instantly embarking. Moreover, links with the M11 and Canary Wharf made access easy.

For several years London City Airport ran at a loss. It had accumulated debts of more than £50 million by 1995, when it was sold to the Dublin businessman Dermot Desmond for £25.5 million. By this time, however, four-engined BAe146 jets, which replaced the earlier twin-prop planes, were able to reach from here any major European city within a range of 1,600 kilometres (1,000 miles). Also the runway was extended, and the airport's profitability began to turn the corner in 1997. In March of that year the number of passengers increased by 69 per cent compared with the number in March 1996. By this time 11 airlines were using London City Airport, ten of which were registered on the Continent, while the sole UK-registered one (Air UK) was 45 per cent owned by the Dutch airline KLM.

This was and is the top end of the market. As the Airport Director, John Horne, declared in 1997, 'We like to regard ourselves as the "Dorchester" of airports.' Today there is even a hotel-style, uniformed commissionaire to welcome passengers to London City. By the end of 1998 passengers will reach the airport via the Jubilee Line Extension to Canning Town, and thence a mere 0.8-km (half-mile) ride by airport shuttle. Alternatively, travelling by the Docklands Light Railway offers a quicker shuttle time, buses from the Prince Regent station taking no more than three minutes to reach the terminal.

Below: Enthralling and innovative architecture: a computer-aided design shows an internal view of the entrance canopy of the Jubilee Line Extension, Canary Wharf.

An extension of the Jubilee Line, an idea that had been around since the mid-1960s, marks another major improvement in the transport infrastructure of Docklands. With the signing of the Master Building Agreement between the LDDC and Olympia & York for Canary Wharf in 1987, forecasts of the ultimate number of jobs in the Isle of Dogs dramatically increased. Although the initial DLR was being built to allow for capacity increases, it had not been expected that increased capacity would be needed so quickly, and even the upgrading and extension of the DLR to Bank were not sufficient to guarantee adequate access in the long term. It was clear that another line was needed. In 1988 the LDDC and Olympia & York started discussions about a second Docklands

railway line, initially in the form of an extension of the Bakerloo Line, and later as a new line running from Waterloo to the Greenwich peninsula. These ideas eventually developed under the guidance of London Transport into the Jubilee Line Extension. An important component of the package was a large contribution (£400 million) from Olympia & York towards the costs of the scheme, in recognition of the

Right: A glimpse of the future: the west escape tunnel weaves its way over the new eastbound Jubilee Line Extension running tunnel at Waterloo.

benefits that would arise at Canary Wharf. However, when Olympia & York went into administration in 1992, the project ground to a halt. It was only after the company came out of administration in autumn 1993 and the creditor banks committed to the Olympia & York contribution that the project got back on track.

Left: Art and engineering in harmony: Zadok Ben-David's sculpture *Restless Dream* adorns the western portal of the Limehouse Link tunnel.
Right: The North Quay entrance to the tunnel.

Twin-bore, single-track tunnels cross the Thames four times and connect with eleven brand-new or remodelled stations. In 1998 the Jubilee Line will reach stations in or close by Docklands at London Bridge, at Bermondsey, at Canada Water, at Canary Wharf and at Canning Town. At London Bridge the line will link with the Northern Line. At Canary Wharf and Canning Town the line will link with the Docklands Light Railway. As a result of this extension, Canary Wharf will be just a nine-minute ride from London Bridge. And the stations will remain architectural treats: Canary Wharf's designed by Sir Norman Foster & Partners; Bermondsey, by Ian Ritchie Associates; Canning Town, by Troughton McAslan.

The final 'push' in regenerating Docklands' transport infrastructure was the creation of a series of new highways, designed to provide 24 kilometres (15 miles) of new roads with improved capacity, from Limehouse in the west to the Royals in the east. The inadequacy of the roads in Docklands was underlined when the Docklands Joint Committee published proposals for a Docklands Northern Relief Road through Limehouse with a scheme finally adopted by the GLC in 1978. While the GLC agreed with the LDDC on the need for the DLR, the two authorities could not agree on the priority of the road schemes. By 1986, and the abolition of the GLC, the LDDC had approved the acquisition of land for the construction of access roads known as the Docklands highways – a series of dual carriageways south of the A13, designed to connect the City to the Isle of Dogs, the Royal Docks and on to the national motorway network. Royal Docks Road connected the A13/A406 to the Gallions roundabout at the eastern end of the Royal Docks. A new road – Royal Albert Way – was built across the north side of the Albert Dock, with the Beckton extension of the DLR running between its two carriageways for a good part of its length. With the railway it was designed to serve the development sites in the area and to make the vast expanses of the Royal Docks attractive to investors and developers. The old Connaught Swing Bridge running north-side between the Royal Victoria and Royal Albert Docks was replaced by a new bridge and North Woolwich Road widened. Bridging the

River Lea, the new Lower Lea Crossing bridge connects to the new Aspen Way and the route of Docklands North Relief Road proposal. The East India Dock Tunnel was built connecting Aspen Way to the A13, the westbound connection waiting for completion of major improvements to the A13 by government due early next century.

The key to the whole new road network was the Limehouse Link, a new dual carriageway tunnel under the Limehouse Basin, providing a connection from Aspen Way at North Quay and Westferry Road on the west side of the island to The Highway, Wapping, and the City of London. Reg Ward, who was a key player in the development of the scheme, remembers that no one postulated what the level of traffic would be or what would happen to that traffic when it reached Tower Bridge. But the Department

of Transport and the Department of the Environment were persuaded of its necessity, the latter in the end footing the bill for this and the remainder of the Docklands highways through the LDDC. The £250 million scheme was unveiled in late 1986, work started on the site in 1989 and the road opened to traffic in May 1993, meaning that the Link was planned and built in seven years, compared with the average for a Department of Transport highway scheme of 13 years. When it opened, LDDC Chairman Michael Pickard described it as 'a major boost to confidence in London Docklands', one that provided 'the final proof that the area is one of the most accessible in the capital'.

But the path was not always a smooth one. Understandably many local people, particularly those living in or near the line of the new roads, opposed the plans. To

minimize the amount of demolition in this residential area a serpentine route was chosen for the tunnel, under Limehouse Basin and linking parcels of derelict, underused and cleared land. The underground route also allowed the land above the tunnel to be redeveloped and removed traffic congestion from the area, while the 'cut and cover' design minimized disruption during construction as once the tunnel roof was in place, construction activity took place underground. The LDDC was not a highways authority, and thus needed the co-operation of the Newham and Tower Hamlets Councils. When Michael Honey succeeded as Chief Executive of the LDDC in May 1988, part of his remit from the then Secretary of State for the Environment, Nicholas Ridley, was to pursue the transport policies of the LDDC, while simultaneously knitting the corporation into the local communities and building bridges with the local

authorities. Honey believes that his previous local government experience, as Chief Executive of Richmond, made him particularly qualified for this. He also professed skills in social housing, in education, and in the provision of recreational facilities and training. With these skills the future of the LDDC looked bright. The Corporation's pioneering agreement with Tower Hamlets Council, the Accord (see chapter 3), was a milestone in LDDC/community relations: in return for the council's promise not to obstruct the LDDC's transport plans and to release public land for the purposes of road construction, the LDDC pledged to rehouse council tenants who would be affected by the work, and to fund a £35 million package of social, economic and community initiatives to benefit Tower Hamlets' residents. It is worth noting that in Newham, where road construction was to take place on mostly derelict land, a less formal contract known as the Memorandum of Agreement sufficed, and in Southwark, where infrastructure works were minimal, no agreement was necessary.

Michael Honey's successor, Eric Sorensen, came to the LDDC from the Department of the Environment, where his career had included taking responsibility for its urban policy and for inner city regeneration. He stayed at the LDDC till March 1997, when he became Chief Executive of the Millennium Commission. The new transport structure he inherited was vital for the regeneration of Docklands, not only to enable residents to take advantage of new housing and unprecedented work opportunities, but also to enable those living outside the area to get there with ease.

Under Sorensen's leadership the LDDC continued to improve such links. A series of footbridges were built to span the sometimes vast expanses of dock water. Designed by collaborations of architects and engineers and chosen by competition, the footbridges offer stylish and innovative solutions to crossing the waters of Docklands. For example, in May

Left: Royal Albert Way and the other new Docklands roads have greatly improved access to the area. The seemingly ubiquitous unmanned trains of the Docklands Light Railway glide above the scene.
Right: South Quay, once the site of a concrete and barrel-vaulted warehouse, is now filled with offices, restaurants and shops. Fittingly, in view of the past, its footbridge displays nautical features.

1997 a new footbridge was opened at South Quay, offering access to Canary Wharf and its Jubilee Line station from the residential and business areas to the south. Shaped like the letter S, the bridge has a span of 180 metres (590 feet) and can be moved to accommodate future development. Work on a footbridge with a span of 127.5 metres (418 feet) across the Royal Victoria Dock to join up the Custom House Docklands Light Railway station with the West Silvertown Urban Village will be completed by the end of 1997.

In 1994 it was found that almost 50 per cent of the 1 million plus people who had visited Docklands the previous year were day trippers from London and the south-east. They included school parties, senior

citizens' groups and women's institutes. The Docklands Light Railway had just opened its Beckton extension. Rainbow Holidays voted Scandic Crown Hotel (now the Holiday Inn Nelson Dock) 'Newcomer Hotel of the Year'. The once-despised area was attracting enormous interest. As a result, the English Bus London Pride tour was started up, its open-top buses running from Lower Regent Street for a two-hour tour of Docklands. Since the service operated every half-hour, passengers could hop off one bus to visit a preferred site, and hop on the next one.

For those Docklanders and visitors who prefer simply to bus, walk or cycle around the neighbourhood, the LDDC decided to use its muscle to provide safe pedestrian walks. There are also more than 60 kilometres (37 miles) of safe and attractive cycle paths. The LDDC insisted that any new developments allowed members of the public access to the river and dock edge. St Saviour's footbridge and Limekiln Dock footbridge, both funded by the LDDC, also helped to improve pedestrian routes. And, as LDDC's Marketing Director Sunny Crouch put it, 'Attracting visitors to an area is a very important contribution to urban regeneration.' So a further initiative from the LDDC was to contribute to the Countryside Commission's Thames Path route, by providing signposts along the 8-kilometre (5-mile) stretch from Tower Bridge to Greenwich.

Today motorists approaching the Limehouse Link tunnel from the west are greeted by a sculpture, created by Zadok Ben-David, entitled 'Restless Dream'. It was commissioned by the LDDC in 1992 along with two other sculptures adorning the tunnel at North Quay and Westferry Road, and is affixed to the Limehouse Link's western portal. Its 9-metre (30-foot) disc portrays black, silhouetted figures which are joined together in a web, inside which floats a giant, sleeping, two-dimensional man. But Docklands is no longer asleep (if it ever was) and far from two-dimensional. And as a result of the initiatives outlined here, it is now readily accessible.

Above right: **Riverside pathways, such as this one at Canada Water, have been created by the LDDC.**

Far right: **Entrancing St Saviour's Dock, with its cranes and converted warehouses, is reached by a footbridge which links Butlers Wharf with New Concordia Wharf.**

7

Out of the smoke and noise and sin
    The heart of the poet cried:
'O God! but to be Thy labourer there,
    On the gentle hill's green side –
To leave the struggle of want and wealth,
    And the battle of lust and pride!'

C. W. Earle

A Glimpse into the Future

Opposite: **A dramatic perspective: looking through Poplar Footbridge, with One Canada Square in the background.**

C W. Earle's lines, from her *Pot-Pourri from a Surrey Garden*, quote the young wife of a clergyman who worked hard amid what Mrs Earle called 'the sordid blackness of a manufacturing town' on the banks of a river. By the late 1990s, the greening of London Docklands was well under way. Docklands was neither sordid nor black.

Ironically, some of the people involved from the start in the regeneration of Docklands through the LDDC were now involved in the closure of the Corporation. And as the LDDC's last Chairman, Sir Michael Pickard, has noted, 'It is no easy task to work yourself selflessly out of a job, yet that is what many of our people have been doing during the year.'

'The LDDC is a short-life organization,' Stephanie Williams had observed in 1990. 'Its job as a catalyst is almost done.' What will happen next? she asked. Who will move there? From where? 'Will the offices that we are building today, this vast expansion of the City eastward, founder in the same way as the docks, conceived and built on the crest of a wave of demand?'

By 1997 the demand was even greater. Docklands was not foundering. Flats with a view of the river were commanding up to £340 per 0.9 square metres (1 square foot). Non-riverside flats were commanding around £250. In 1997 Barratt Homes, which began building on

Docklands in 1982, had 100 homes on offer at Prince's Riverside, one-bedroom flats costing £99,000. At Gallions View the same company offered 67 flats, two-bedroom ones costing nearly £150,000. Similar developments by the same company had been completed or proposed at Victoria Wharf, at Pierhead Lock, at Pageant Steps, at Sovereign View, at Regents Landing and at Brunswick Wharf. But, as has been seen, Barratt was not the sole major developer in this housing regeneration. Berkeley, followed by Wimpey, by Regalian, by Bellway and by Fairview among others, were busy exploiting the new demand east of the city.

But on 31 March 1998 the LDDC will close down, in spite of efforts to persuade the government to extend its remit to the year 2000. 'Thereafter the local municipalities will be faced with the challenge to build on existing achievements,' Peter Turlik observes. Unparalleled opportunities still exist for linking private enterprise with an outstanding degree of public commitment. He adds: 'The goal is to complete the work of regeneration in a way that makes London Docklands a model for urban life, and sets the standards by which all such future enterprises will be judged in the twenty-first century.' Former Chief Executive Eric Sorensen, for one, believes that there is enough momentum for the initiatives of the LDDC to prosper in future years. (He wryly comments, 'In a year's time we'll not be here to take any blame.')

Left: A glimpse of the future: an artist's impression of the design for phase 1 of the Canary Wharf Riverside scheme.

Below: Baltic Quay, a residential complex built in 1990, overlooks South Dock marina.

In Beckton the LDDC agreed a withdrawal package with Newham Council that involved, for instance, £1.2 million to help fund a new Royal Docks Trust. This will enable the Trust to continue to operate community grants in the future. To improve East Beckton District Centre, more cash has been made available to the Borough of Newham for the creation of a multi-purpose building. The LDDC and the council set up these arrangements with a formal 'Statement of Agreed Intentions'.

David Anstey, who was seconded from the LDDC to work as Docklands Project Manager for the London Borough of Newham, says: 'From the council's point of view, the need is to carry on the vision of the LDDC for the Royal Docks.' Newham Council, he observes, is very supportive of the plans for the exhibition centre on the north side of the Royal Docks, which will not only bring benefits for local businesses but will also provide new employment, some of it probably for local people. Although there are uncertainties over funding, if the project succeeds it will have enormous benefits for supporting businesses and will aid supplying industries moving into the borough.

In addition, Anstey points out, the new Docklands campus for the University of East London will complement the borough's other educational programmes. The project will fit in with nearby businesses, for the university's emphasis will be on technology. This too is part of the regeneration of the area, making sure that people will come and perhaps stay because the educational standards of Newham are excellent.

Furthermore, the university will be a major civic building, and as such, it was decided, should be architecturally fascinating. Edward Cullinan Architects were appointed to design it. As Professor Frank Gould, Vice-Chancellor of the University of East London, said, 'We are looking for a stunning building.' The first students will arrive on the campus in September 1999.

The council, too, says David Anstey, is supportive of the Norton Healthcare headquarters, which will house a pharmaceutical company moving from Harlow to the north side of Albert Basin, bringing with it some 400 staff. In the long term this will generate local employment. Norton Healthcare, a subsidiary of the American Ivax Corporation, plans a complex of 28,900 square metres (311,000 square feet), including a product selection and packaging plant. With the University it will be part of a Business Park, along the length of Royal Albert Dock, which the LDDC promoted during its final year.

As for West Silvertown Urban Village, some 16 hectares (40 acres) of development land is still available. The LDDC and Newham Council envisage for this a high-quality mixed development: the first phase of development, which is well under way, is the building of 1,000 houses and flats for sale and for rent, while the second phase will see the creation of commercial and leisure facilities focused on the Pontoon Dock at the eastern end of the site, as well as more new homes.

Below: A model of Royal Victoria Dock footbridge, which connects West Silvertown Urban Village to DLR stations on the north side of the dock.

Not every decision is an easy one.
A planning application has been lodged to expand flights from London City Airport. The obvious benefits this would bring have to be balanced with the environmental aspects of such an expansion, and with the effect it might have on the local community. But David Anstey confirms that this remains part of the council's vision for the area.

'The council sees the next stage as integrating the Royals with the regeneration of the rest of the borough,' he says. The Royals he perceives as giving a new image to Newham. 'It defines what are the benefits of coming to work in Newham. It will bring in investment.' He adds: 'It will also add to the pride of the local residents.'

As for Bermondsey Riverside, the LDDC is convinced that the area will continue to be supported by Southwark Council to play its unique role in the future shape and function of Central London. 'Its architectural richness will continue to be protected and enhanced by sensitive traffic-management schemes which will enable pleasurable and safe pedestrian exploration.' The LDDC declared that the contribution that the area can make to stimulating the riverfront, to increased use of river transport, and to an expansion of retailing on the south bank are matters that the council will actively pursue in tandem with local commercial and residential interests. 'Together with its local partners,' the LDDC concluded, 'Southwark Council will realize the goal of fulfilling the area's potential and integrating it as a pearl in the crown of Central London.'

As the London Borough of Southwark took over much of the work of the LDDC in that part of Docklands, Fred Manson, the borough's Director of Regeneration and Environment, judged that 'the Corporation has been very useful, and has achieved a lot of things'. He added, 'Now it is time to take regeneration back to social issues, and to see that democratic bodies carry on the long development of what the LDDC started.'

In the 1990s the LDDC increasingly began to monitor its own performance. For example Travel and Tourism Research Ltd found that in 1996 more than 1.6 million people visited Docklands. Their visits injected £7 million into Docklands' economy. They came 'to look around generally', to absorb the waterside

atmosphere, and above all to see the architecture. These tourists were for the most part young and middle-class. The chief attractions were Canary Wharf, St Katharine Docks, Hay's Galleria, Butlers Wharf, the London Docklands Visitor Centre and Island Gardens, with its renowned view of Greenwich and the Royal Observatory.

In a further monitoring of its performance, the LDDC commissioned surveys from MORI, aimed at gauging the attitudes of local residents to the Corporation. Firstly, the surveys aimed to measure the residents' views of the work of the Corporation. Secondly, they attempted to gauge the LDDC's reputation both for informing and for consulting residents. MORI was also asked to explore the readership and ratings of the LDDC publication *Docklands News*. Good and bad aspects of living in Docklands were to be researched. MORI was also asked to find out how local communities had benefited from the actions of the LDDC. Key services – transport, housing, education and health – were to be rated. Finally, MORI was commissioned to ask the residents about their most needed services and their priorities for the future.

The 1996 survey discovered that on every aspect the image of the LDDC had improved since 1994. Those living in Surrey Docks were particularly pleased, whereas the residents of the Royal Docks and the Isle of Dogs were less so. Those living in the Royal Docks were markedly more critical.

MORI pointed out that these attitudes were in part related to demographic factors, noting that old East End communities, which were predominantly white, working-class or unemployed, people who had lived in the area for a long time, were more critical of the LDDC. Yet even here, the majority took a positive line, while those coming to live in the area were even more appreciative of what had been achieved.

Right above: **A model showing development at West India Quay, Isle of Dogs.**
Far right: **Thomas More Square, reflected in the water of St Katharine Docks, Wapping.**

Below: Another glimpse of the future: the proposed Thames Gateway Crossing at Gallions Reach.

Naturally enough, residents were concerned about unemployment, vandalism and crime, about facilities for young people, about traffic, about shopping facilities and about the environment. Nevertheless, many had become increasingly satisfied with the quality of life in Docklands, particularly with regard to employment, crime prevention, public transport, medical facilities (i.e. doctors and clinics) and the benefits brought by the Docklands Light Railway – in the view of many, a major plus in the Urban Development Area, even though most residents still use buses as their normal means of transport (a service much invested in by the LDDC). They wanted still more shops and leisure facilities, more retailers, better traffic control, more public transport initiatives and opportunities for young people.

In fact, the LDDC had already stimulated numerous provisions for leisure activities for the young. For example early in 1995 the Corporation donated £700,000 to set up, with Tower Hamlets Council, an all-weather sports pitch at George Green Secondary School and a teenagers' recreational area at St Andrew's Wharf, with a running track, climbing frames, an aerial rope walk and so on. Another delightfully bizarre initiative, aimed in 1995 at nursery children, was the 'sensory

trail' at Surrey Docks Farm. Sights, smells and tastes were all involved. Children tasted honey, listened to ducks and poultry, sniffed herbs, felt fur and bristles and looked at feathers. They also sat on 'feely' bags – soft, prickly and rough. In the same year, in co-operation with the 25-year-old Newham Riding School and Association, the LDDC also sponsored a new Equestrian Centre, close by Sainsbury's Savacentre in Beckton, as a home for the Docklands Pony Club and Newham Riding for the Disabled. Its facilities included stabling for 17 horses and ponies, a livery stable, an indoor arena and parking for 55 cars.

Altogether, not surprisingly, two out of three residents in Docklands believed that the LDDC had done a good job, and 23 per

cent of the population held that the Corporation had done a very good job. Health centres and dental practices, two services supported and stimulated by the LDDC over its years, were much appreciated, though many residents were dissatisfied with regard to hospitals and the care for elderly people.

Many residents felt that their area would worsen after the LDDC's involvement ended. They feared there would be less money available. They worried about how the local authorities would manage.

In February 1997 the *London Evening Standard* voiced some of their fears. Residents felt that the LDDC was 'about to leave them in the lurch'. Regeneration might be transformed into stagnation, new life turn into decay. One community leader, Richard Roberts of Limehouse (whose commitment to the area included service as Vice-Chairman of Limehouse Youth Club and as Chairman of the Barley Mow tenants' association), was quoted as saying, 'The LDDC is pulling the plug too soon.' (In truth, the government had pulled the plug.) He observed that some 1,200 homes were being built in Limehouse, eagerly snapped up by people longing to move in. But he asked how long that would last if the money were to be cut off.

Roberts also wondered about the future of Ropemakers Field, a park with tennis courts, greens and a bandstand. The LDDC spent £45,000 a year on its maintenance. Now Tower Hamlets had a mere £10,000 to keep it in good shape. As Roberts rightly (and colourfully) put it, 'It's a wonderful area, but if there is not the money for its upkeep it will go back to what it was before, a bleak, flat area that was used as a dog toilet.'

At times the development of Docklands had been a close-run affair. The task had been a complex one – in Reg Ward's words, 'that of creative management of change'. He went on: 'Achieving the right balance between housing and industry and facilities for leisure, ensuring that the new landscape matches the quality of the waterscape' – all these were the pieces which fitted into the jigsaw of the 'exceptional place'.

Regeneration, too, had to cope with the vagaries of the economic climate. In 1992 Professor S. K. Al Naib (head of the department of civil engineering at the University of East London) described Canary Wharf as 'the jewel in Docklands' crown'. So it was, and is; but after its developer, Olympia & York, was taken into administration, much else faltered. One casualty was RiverBus, whose chief backer

Olympia & York had been. This was a service whose eight catamarans and two executive launches had once carried as many as 750,000 passengers a year. Since 1993, as we have seen, there has been no real substitute.

A much scaled-down service has emerged. One impetus is the Millennium Experience, the exhibition planned to open beside the Thames on the Greenwich peninsula. Another impetus was the change of government in 1997. The new Deputy Prime Minister John Prescott took on a brief to persuade people to leave their cars at home. Nick Raynsford, the Minister for London and MP for Greenwich, urged a 'much better use of the river as a transport artery', adding that the Thames should be opened up for public use. And Canary Wharf was once again alive and well. In February 1997 ground was broken there on its thirteenth tower block: a new corporate headquarters for Citibank, designed by Sir Norman Foster. The following summer work started on new homes and a hotel on the riverside at Canary Wharf.

Eric Sorensen had taken over as Chief Executive at a time when dialogue between the LDDC and the local authorities was low. 'We just sat there in trenches and lobbed mortars at each other,' he remembered. In his view, the Accord with Tower Hamlets and the Memorandum of Agreement with Newham ought to have been in place on Day One of the beginning of the Docklands quango.

Right: **Lavender Pond is a prime example of urban ecology, serving as a nature reserve sheltering both wildlife and plants.**

Sorensen's aim when he arrived was to build up new confidence, above all between the Corporation and the Department of the Environment. But he also had views on what still needed to be achieved in the last decade of the LDDC's life. Improving the environment was one priority. The place, he believed, looked untidy and unkempt. To put this right, Eric Sorensen believed, would generate local pride.

In spite of the public relations work of the LDDC (including its glossy newspaper *Docklands News*) press coverage of the Corporation's work was often negative. It was suggested that Docklands' growth was shambolic, with no thought given to planning and design. When the housing boom collapsed, many critics considered their adverse judgements vindicated. Eric Sorensen was determined to prove them wrong. Docklands needed a positive image.

Advertising, he believed, was not enough to achieve this. 'I am always fairly cynical about advertising,' he averred. Docklands, he said, was not a brand image. But when it came to the tourist attractions and leisure facilities, as well as the ecology and the flora and fauna of the region, then perceptions might change. So, slowly, under the guidance of its Chief Executive, the walls of hostility and indifference to Docklands were breached.

Right above: **London's business heart expands eastwards: the new Citibank office at Canary Wharf.**
Far right:
Regenerated East India Dock with its elegant waterside walkway.

In 1997 Sorensen left, to become Chief Executive of the Millennium Commission. As LDDC Chairman Sir Michael Pickard commented, 'Eric Sorensen has done a tremendous job for London Docklands over the last six years.' Sir Michael also noted that the Corporation had consistently supported the notion of a Millennium Exhibition at Greenwich, adding, 'We believe it will provide the impetus for continued major investment in the East End of London.'

As he departed, Eric Sorensen commented, 'I shall miss people here, and the liveliness of the East End.' He added: 'The pace of development is strong and there is much more variety bringing new life to the area. The prospects here are very good.'

Left: Transport in
Docklands – a
computer-aided
design of the Jubilee
Line Extension
station at Canary
Wharf.

Two men took over from him at the LDDC,
as joint Chief Executives whose job it
would be to take the Corporation to
the end of its remit. Both men had
considerable experience of the LDDC.
Neil Spence had joined the Corporation as
Director of Finance in 1989. Roger Squire,
his fellow joint Chief Executive, joined the
LDDC in 1991 as Assistant Chief Executive,
Development.

In its remaining months the LDDC devoted
most of its attention to the Royal Docks.
Detailed plans involved the development
of London's new exhibition centre.
Planning permission was obtained in
February 1996, and the first phase,
designed for a 40-hectare (100-acre) site
on the north side of Royal Victoria Dock,
was planned to be finished in 1999 after
the projected completion of the Jubilee
Line Extension. In 1996 it was estimated
that the fully completed exhibition centre
would attract more than 2.8 million
visitors annually, generating over 14,000
new jobs.

The second major project is the proposed
University of East Docklands campus on
Royal Albert Dock, designed for 5,000
students, with enrolment beginning, it is
hoped, in 1999. At its heart is the Thames
Gateway Technology Centre, which was
given a boost of £7.8 million from the
government's Single Regeneration
Challenge Fund. Thames Gateway
Technology Centre aims to offer a
range of services for new and existing
manufacturing companies in East London,

training staff to the highest standards
and offering the companies product
development and research.

Meanwhile the Corporation was closing
down, or de-designating, as the jargon is.
In October 1994 Bermondsey Riverside
was de-designated and handed on to the
London Borough of Southwark. In
December the following year Beckton was
handed on to the London Borough of
Newham. Surrey Docks had been returned
to the London Borough of Southwark in
December 1996. Wapping and Limehouse
were handed on to the London Borough of
Tower Hamlets in January 1997.

The Surrey Docks peninsula had been part
of the remit of the LDDC for over 15 years.
The local authority now inherited such
assets as the dock estate, Surrey Docks
Farm, Surrey Quays Shopping Centre and
development sites at Canada Water Jubilee
Line Station, though some of these assets
were not finally transferred till mid-1997.
Meanwhile developers had completed work
on the £20 million Canada Water retail
park, the largest scheme south of the river
negotiated by the LDDC since 1987. On an
adjacent site a major leisure complex is
under construction.

Since July 1981 more than 5,500 new
homes had been built including 1,500
housing association properties. Yet
another grant of £10.5 million had helped
in the refurbishment of 1,500 council
homes. In Timber Pond Road, Bacon's
College (the area's first secondary school)

In the following month a similar Statement of Agreed Intentions was signed with Tower Hamlets Council, to which Wapping and Limehouse were handed on. Some £350,000 was committed by the LDDC for social housing and future refurbishment. Another £440,000 was pledged for improving the social and community infrastructure of Wapping.

had been founded, partly funded by an LDDC grant of £3.5 million and in co-operation with the Church of England, the government and the Sir Philip and Lady Harris Trust. Another £1 million had been spent by the Corporation on three new primary schools. Nearly half a million pounds had been donated to the Surrey Quays annex of Southwark College. Health centres, ecological parks (such as the 2.2-hectare (5½-acre) one at Stave Hill), a 250-berth marina, new roads and walkways had all been stimulated by the LDDC. The population had risen from just under 6,000 in 1981 to around 16,000.

In December 1996 Southwark Council committed itself to a 'Statement of Agreed Intentions' with the LDDC, in which the council pledged itself to maintain such features as Canada Water, Greenland Dock, Surrey Docks and several open spaces, as well as the walkways. As for the LDDC, its Chief Executive, Eric Sorensen, declared, 'The LDDC has much to be proud of in Surrey Docks. In 1981 the infilled dock space we inherited showed little promise of things to come. Employment was sparse and housing was run down.' Now, he concluded, 'The future of the area is very bright.'

Once again, in the years of the LDDC, the population had risen – though not so much as in Southwark, significantly – from some 5,200 to over 10,500. Wapping and Gill Street health centres had been substantially improved. And one major, innovative development, funded to the tune of £1.2 million by the LDDC, had been the establishment of the Eva Armsby Centre, whose purpose is to support vulnerable children and their families. Nursery provision was stimulated by the LDDC. And Limehouse Youth Club was built at a cost of £1.2 million. Yet the LDDC did not simply concentrate on the young: it spent £293,000 to help future refurbishment of the Barley Mow Veterans' Club.

Nonetheless, no one pretends that problems no longer exist here, or that with the closure of the LDDC they will not in some respects be exacerbated. Tim Chudleigh, East of Borough Manager, is quite open about them. Many social problems still exist, for as he observes, 'With the LDDC social regeneration always came secondary to physical regeneration.' A recent survey revealed that 40 per cent of heads of households in the borough thought that the prospect of housing was getting worse, not better. Nor do people yet think of Tower Hamlets as providing labour, though this is a relatively poor area which needs new jobs. And now the major source of cash is to dry up.

Chudleigh's authority is not, however, short of initiatives. With the other major players in the area – obviously Canary Wharf, but also the other Lea Valley boroughs and Lea Valley Partnership, as well as the London First organization – there ought to be a strong possibility of continuing to promote the area, though not of course to the tune of the LDDC's annual marketing budget of some £4 million. Should there soon be a strategic government for London, plus a Lord Mayor, that will be another great boost.

In October 1997 the LDDC passed on its responsibilities on the Isle of Dogs to Tower Hamlets. The council and the LDDC agreed to spend £1 million on community activities and facilities over the following three years, while a further £2 million endowment was made by the LDDC to the Isle of Dogs Community Foundation to allow the foundation to undertake a substantial long-term programme of grants for community activities. The council took responsibility for the Corporation's public open spaces; river wall and walkways. Maintenance in part would be offset by income from the freehold of a Granada Travelodge being built at East India Dock.

Left: **A wind pump, another symbol of ecological care, at Canada Water, Surrey Docks.**

British Waterways, already owners of the nearby Limehouse Basin, took over the West India and Millwall Docks on the Isle of Dogs, receiving the LDDC's interests in the sites of Westferry Printers and West India Quay to offset the costs of the docks' upkeep. Arrangements were agreed for local residents, businesses and users of the water to be consulted on the docks' management through a consultative forum.

In the Royal Docks, Newham Council and English Partnerships would continue what the LDDC started, the latter assuming responsibility for on-going financial commitments and contracts and for the disposal of the remaining LDDC land holdings.

Under the leadership of the LDDC, much of Docklands has risen again, a far cry from the time when, in the delightful words of its first Chief Executive, Reg Ward, 'the area had fewer attractions than a Siberian salt-mine – and the sight of a private investor was as rare as a unicorn.'

The whole team at LDDC has achieved a transformation of East London. 'If Docklands is to have a future, the focus of London – with new roads, railways and underground lines – must move east,' wrote Stephanie Williams in 1990. The LDDC ensured that this has happened. The momentum cannot be stopped. Docklands will continue to thrive.

Right: **Docklands lit up at night. The future is equally bright.**

Bibliography

Al Naib, S. K., *Discover London Docklands*, Ashmead Press, 4th edition, 1994

Al Naib, S. K., *London Docklands, Past, Present and Future*, Ashmead Press, 5th edition, 1993

Beckton, London Docklands Development Corporation, March 1997

Bermondsey Riverside, London Docklands Development Corporation, 1996

Bianco, Anthony, *The Reichmanns: Family, Faith, Fortune and the Empire of Olympia & York*, 1997

Blyth, Robert S., *The Limehouse Link Tunnel: The Planning and Route of the Link*, Proceedings of the Institution of Civil Engineers, 1994

Docklands, An Illustrated Historical Survey of Life and Work in East London, Thames & Hudson, 1986

Docklands' Heritage, London Docklands Development Corporation, 1987

Docklands News, the newspaper of the London Docklands Development Corporation

Ellmers, Chris, and Werner, Alex, *Dockland Life: A Pictorial History of London's Docks 1860–1970*, Mainstream Publishing, 1991

Initiating Urban Change: London Docklands Before the LDDC, London Docklands Development Corporation, 1997

London Docklands: A Decade of Achievement 1981–1991, London Docklands Development Corporation, 1991

Starting from Scratch: The Development of Transport in London Docklands, London Docklands Development Corporation, 1997

Surrey Docks, London Docklands Development Corporation, 1997

Williams, Stephanie, *Docklands*, Phaidon Architectural Guide, 1993

Many thanks to Vicki Blyth, Peter Turlik and Louisa Knox at the London Docklands Development Corporation for their help in producing this book.

PICTURE CREDITS

The publishers would like to thank the following for their kind permission to reproduce photographs in this book:

Ahrends, Burton and Koralek: 198 (Peter Cook)

Arcaid: pp. 6 (John Stuart Miller); 12 (Alex Bartel); 42 (Richard Bryant); 63 (Dennis Gilbert); 75 (John Stuart Miller); 147 (Richard Bryant); 150 (Richard Bryant); 153 (John Stuart Miller); 155 (Mark Fiennes)

Canary Wharf Limited: pp. 200; 212

Jubilee Line Extension Project: pp. 188 (C.A.D/Architect: Graham Cook); 189 (QA Photos); 214 (C.A.D./ Architect: Graham Cook)

The London Docklands Development Corporation (LDDC): pp. 1, 3, 14; 16; 17; 22; 23; 24-5; 26-7; 28; 32-3; 34; 35; 38 (below); 39; 44; 51; 52; 53; 54; 55; 56; 57; 58; 59; 60; 61; 64; 65; 66; 67; 68; 69; 70; 71; 73; 74; 94; 98; 106; 109; 110; 112; 113; 114; 115; 116; 117; 118; 119; 121; 122; 123; 125; 126; 127; 128; 129; 130; 131; 132; 134; 135; 136; 138-9; 140; 141; 142; 143; 145; 146; 148; 149; 151; 152; 154; 156; 157; 158; 159; 160; 162; 163; 165; 166; 167; 168; 170; 175; 176-7 (Five-star Graphics); 178-9; 180; 181; 182; 185; 186; 187; 190; 191; 194; 195; 196; 197; 202; 203; 204; 205; 207; 208; 209; 211; 213; 216; 218-9

Museum in Docklands, PLA Collection: pp. 18; 21; 29; 31; 36; 37; 38 (above); 45; 46-7; 49; 102-3; 104; 105; 172; 173

QA Photos: pp. 93; 192; 193

Mike Seaborne: pp. 19; 30; 40; 41; 48 (for the Island History Trust); 50; 76; 78-9; 80-81 (for the Island History Trust); 82; 84; 85; 86; 87; 89; 90; 95; 96; 97; 100; 101; 107; 108; 120; 124; 174; 184

Michael Squire & Partners: p. 206

Acknowledgements